And He Called Her WOMAN:
Fearfully and Wonderfully MADE

MINISTER JOANN SHEALEY
and Contributing Author
Dr. TOMEKA W. MCGHEE

Cover Design by Taminko J. Kelley of CoolBird Publishing House
Goodwater, AL.

AND HE CALLED HER WOMAN: FEARFULLY AND WONDERFULLY MADE

Published by CoolBird Publishing House
PO Box 612
Goodwater, AL 35072
www.coolbirdmarketing.com

ISBN: 9781096469865
Printed in the United States of America

The material contained in this book is provided for informational purposes only. It is not intended to diagnose, provide advice, or take the place of marital counseling from licensed professionals. Neither the publisher nor the author is responsible for any possible consequences from any person reading or following the information in this book.

And He Called Her WOMAN: Fearfully and Wonderfully MADE

MINISTER JOANN SHEALEY
and Contributing Author
Dr. TOMEKA W. MCGHEE

This book is dedicated to all my sisters who were willing to "Go There" ...Yes, to those places where you were judged, criticized and labeled. Thanks for trusting me enough to share your stories, despite the pain. It's your tears which fueled my pen.

TABLE OF CONTENTS

PART I: Lesson 1 – 10 | Fearfully and Wonderfully Made

PART II: Lesson 11 - 18 | Broken Images

PART III: Lesson 19 - 23 | All Things New

Acknowledgments
from
Minister JoAnn Shealey

To My Heavenly Father- ALL Honor, Glory and Praise to God! How humbling to think that You would trust me with Your Gifts. May You find pleasure in the work of my hands!

To My Husband- I have much gratitude to my Boaz, Larry who affords me the opportunity to glean from his fields of knowledge, steadfastness in the gospel, and sense of purpose. How grateful I am of your love, protection, and support.

To My Children- Larrecia, my daughter and teacher who helps me understand the necessity of clarity and intentional thought, as you meet me often from scattered places. Larry Jr., (Prince Shealey) you have been most valuable. I was "searching for self" as you termed it- though I thought it to be abandonment; which guided me to pen this manuscript with such depth and truth.

To My Siblings- It was our weekly phone gatherings which reminded me of where we've been. It was through each of you that I was able to revisit our past, appreciate each moment, person, and event which has profoundly shaped who we've become. Joe thanks for allowing me to not only share your birthdate, but part of your soul. Truly, I am your offspring. Through your teaching I've learned to see the "sunshine."

To My Spiritual Mother- Syl, my spiritual mother who bore the pain of bringing forth a religious prodigal, who taught me how to slip in the back door of the soul without anyone recognizing I was even in their house.

To My Extended Family - I appreciate my extended family, especially my Uncle Lee Troy, who was brave enough to leave in search of more. To my many cousins who struggle to emerge, thanks for being authentic enough to just live.

To My Church Family- I want to acknowledge the encouragement, patience, and compassion I receive from my church family. I'm especially grateful for Dr. T.W. McGhee, the iron which sharpens and smooths my edges. I'm grateful for your insightful contributions to the book.

Thanks, Sandra for allowing your presence and our differences to challenge me to fight to be authentic and purposeful in God- You are a Gift to the Body of Christ.

Thanks to Sheere Billups, who had the courage and boldness to challenge life's perceptions and "Just Be." It's her continual encouragement from the grave…that allows me to trust in the message. May you rest in peace See you later, my dear friend.

To My Publisher- Thanks, Taminko J. Kelley for enhancing this project with your insights and genius. It was your encouragement to just write without editing and inclusion of worries which allowed me the freedom to flow uninhibited in reaching the deadline for getting this message out.

Acknowledgments
from
Dr. Tomeka W. McGhee

To My Heavenly Father- There is none like You! Anything good in me, You created. Anything good I have, You gave it. You've never left me or forsaken me.

To My Husband- Thank you for always believing I could do anything. Thanks for being open to and giving me space to discover myself and the plan He has for me and us. Thank you for being solid, steady, and trusting which gave me freedom and peace to pursue God's call and plan for my life and our family life. God taught me what generosity, kindness, and unconditional love looks like through you.

To My Children- There's no call or assignment I take more seriously than or above you. Your father and you are my first ministry. Gabriel, Nicolas, and Trinity, I have loved you since the moment I learned you were coming, and I'll fiercely love you until the day I no longer exist.

To My Extended Family- There's a lot of you – Leonard's, Barris', McGhees, McKinney's! I can't possibly name all the names and won't. Just know, I've loved you, prayed for you and am very fond of you as people. Nevertheless, I'd be remiss to not mention the two women who've significantly impacted and influenced my life. These women are the epitome of resilience, strength, fortitude, and leadership. They love deeply and "put up with" little to nothing!

To My beautiful and fabulous mother, Sharon L. McKinney, and my grandmother, Roberta L. Brager - You rock!

To My earthly Dads, Harry Barris and Naman McKinney- I've learned much from watching and experiencing you… to take it easy, accept what comes in life with humor, own your mistakes, and forgiveness. To my best friend of 26 years, Dorothy L. Martin, who has seen and heard it all! You are one of the pillars of my strength and without *every single* conversation we've had I wouldn't be where I am with confidence… and sanity. Love you girl!

To My Church Family- There are so many people to which I consider to be my church family. Whether it's where I received my initial training and developed my love for God and His people, New Home, or where I've done the bulk of my ministry work, Darian, or individuals who've made an indelible mark in my spiritual life, Minister JoAnn Shealey, Pastor Larry D. Shealey, and Rev. Lathonia Wright, thank you!

And He Called Her WOMAN:
Fearfully and Wonderfully MADE

MINISTER JOANN SHEALEY
and Contributing Author
Dr. TOMEKA W. MCGHEE

Thank you to the many women who invested in the development of this project. It was your encouragement that allowed me to believe that I had a message worthy of print...That encouragement sent me to the pages flowing freely from somewhere and everywhere.

Let's Begin...

PREFACE

There are many types of writing styles and genres. For some authors, writing is a purposeful and, even, exacting, professional or scholarly endeavor. This book is not that. Through the medium of storytelling or narratives, the book incorporates a poetic, expository, and descriptive view of its content. This reflective, Scripture-laced, and, sometimes, raw work is a culmination of a lifetime journey of personal spiritual growth or awakening intertwined with decades of discipleship ministry to women. The uniqueness of this book *is* its raw truths about the genuine and real struggle to "work out your own soul's salvation" in the culture of the Church, in the Bible Belt and rural venue of Alabama, and, more specifically, as a preacher's kid and minister. Rarely do we hear the undressed stories of "wounded healers;" you know, the ones that don't meet the criteria of salaciousness and pilfering necessary for the headlines. Then, certainly, we don't hear many stories in book form of that experience from the cultural perspective of a female in ministry who is not trying to usurp male authority, replace him in leadership, or denounce his importance in the Church, home, and community. While this mixed style of writing offers a glimpse into that culture, also, it brings to light inaccurate and unhealthy messages acquired through familial and church cultural norms that have maimed God-Man, parent-child, and marital relationships as well as produced an intergenerational conflict that was uncommon in the twentieth century. The objective of the book is to acquire truths by going back to Genesis for our original design and looking at subsequent Scripture in light of Christ's example. The objective is to renew the mind to those truths that we might live the life of

14

abundance and peace Christ promised is available to us now and in the life to come. The objective is to realign our way of being to reflect the image of God to which we were created, that we might draw others to Him and prepare ourselves for His second return. This book is a call for us all, but women particularly, to discover who we are by name, give God our broken images and nakedness, allow Him to create something new; then go out, be fruitful, and multiply the image we see in Him using the name He gives us. We acknowledge the complexity and varying positions on the content and issues raised in the book. We further acknowledge that it wasn't our attempt to address every side, perspective, or caveat of said positions or issues in this writing. As professionals with many years of experience in varying areas, we acknowledge that the opinions and experiences of the authors aren't necessarily alike but do agree and stand united in the larger message of having a genuine, authentic, and congruent identity that is God-given and how that identity is to shape our way of being in this earthly experience.

-Tomeka W. McGhee, Ph.D., LPC, NCC, GCDF

INTRODUCTION

Shake Me to Wake Me...

I found myself slipping into a state of unconsciousness. I
was becoming passive, unintentional, and unfruitful. Perhaps
I'd attuned too often the soft lyrics of "no absolutes" and
freedoms the world sang. Then, I was shaken...my inner
man was awakened to give birth to this manuscript.
Although the book appears as one writing, three separate
parts are included. Each part is written with the intent to
show man's progression from God then back to Him. Part
One allows the reader to look at creation. Here, we find a
holy and righteous God consulting with every aspect of
Himself and, thus, deciding that His image would best be
presented through man and woman (Genesis 1:26-27).
Although God could have chosen any other source even
angels to represent His image, He allows man the Honor
(Psalm 8:4-6). Since the earth can only see and know a
spiritual God through man, He gives man a world complete
with everything needed to bring Him Glory. He charges man
to subdue, have dominion, and replenish the earth with those
possessing His image (Genesis 1:28). I believe that it was
God's intent that mankind would live forever as He placed
man in the garden (earth) to tend and keep it. Man and
woman's authority was limited by only one command, they
could eat of every tree in the garden except the one that
would give them knowledge of good and evil. God promised
that death would be imposed should they disobey His
command (Genesis 2:15-17). Man and woman living and
working together to preserve God's glorious image has been
and will throughout eternity be the whole duty of man.

Moses, the great leader and deliverer of God's people from Egypt, served as God's prototype. He warns the remnant Joshua, Caleb, and the children born to those who died in rebellion after 40 years in the wilderness to be careful to teach the commands of God and preserve His image throughout the generations (Deuteronomy 6:1-9). He admonishes them to never forget God as they came into the land promised to Abraham, Isaac, and to Jacob, their fathers... a place of material goods and comforts (Deuteronomy 6:10-12). Part II presents the plight of mankind who now presents a "Broken Image" of God. Sin has separated them from His presence. Although they can hear Him (the Word), they find it difficult to live in obedience to His Word because they lack His presence. As a result, they live with deceptions, conflicts, and resentments. In an attempt to avoid the piercing eyes of their accusers, man and woman retreat deeper and deeper among the trees in search of whatever might cover their nakedness (Genesis 3:7-10). Moses knew God intimately... the Lord spoke to Moses face-to-face as a man speaks to his friend (Exodus 33:11). Although Moses had a close relationship with God, he also knew that God would allow mankind to come into a land filled with His promises and not be with them.

"Then the LORD said to Moses, leave this place, you and the people you brought up out of Egypt, and go up to the land I promised on oath to Abraham, Isaac and Jacob, saying, I will give it to your descendants. I will send an angel before you and drive out the Canaanites, Amorites, Hittites, Perizzites, Hivites and Jebusites. Go up to the land flowing with milk and honey. But I will not go with you, because you are a stiff-necked people and I might destroy you on the way."
Exodus 33:1-3, NIV

Although God called Moses to lead His people, he detests the thought of God possibly sending him to a land of promise without His presence. Although he'd been instrumental in bringing God's people out of Egypt, he knew that it was only because of God's presence with him that he'd been successful. It's at this pivotal point that Moses' character is challenged. Would he lead the people without face-to-face encounters with God? He'd been established as their leader; they knew him only through his witness. How would they discern if God was with him or not? Moses chooses humility and Godly wisdom over earthly knowledge. Thus, God promises Moses His perpetual presence and establishes His covenant with him.

"Moses said to the LORD, you have been telling me, lead these people, but you have not let me know whom you will send with me. You have said, 'I know you by name and you have found favor with me. If you are pleased with me, teach me your ways so I may know you and continue to find favor with you. Remember that this nation is your people. The LORD replied, My Presence will go with you, and I will give you rest." Exodus 33:12-14 (NIV)

We've come into the promises of the land, but I fear we've forfeited God's presence. Far too many leaders have chosen prosperity in exchange for God's presence. Moses affirms his need and reliance for God by saying if you go not up with me then cause us not to go up.

"Then Moses said to him, "If your Presence does not go with us, do not send us up from here." Exodus 33:15 (NIV)

Moses asks God how a world will know Him or His people without His presence. Unfortunately, too many Christians have chosen to "go up" without His presence. Therefore, we are in a world that doubts who God is and who we are in God. No longer can men and women who are called to bear the image of God do so without His presence. God stands in the earth proclaiming "I AM WHO I AM."

When I awoke from my sleep, I found myself crying, saying, "If you do not go with me, then I won't go either." I listen intently to hear Him amid the noise and chaos of a society screaming for various freedoms. He's the still small voice which Moses heard as he hid in the cliff of the rock as God passed in His glory, demonstrating the covenant of presence He'd established with Moses. "Then the LORD said, "There is a place near me where you may stand on a rock. When my glory passes by, I will put you in a cleft in the rock and cover you with my hand until I have passed by. Then I will remove my hand and you will see my back; but my face must not be seen" Exodus 33:21-23 (NIV).

Part III presents the people of God journeying back to God in humility and obedience. They have renounced sinful flesh with its discord and have full assurance in the New Life offered through Christ. Each having returned to oneness with God and each other will be guided by the Holy Spirit (Breath of God) restoring the glorious image of God in the earth. I believe God is preparing the earth for His coming… a time when all will be one in God and each other (John 17:21). We are attempting to offer you hope, deliverance and restoration as you journey through this book.

And He Called Her WOMAN:
Fearfully and Wonderfully MADE

MINISTER JOANN SHEALEY
and Contributing Author
Dr. TOMEKA W. MCGHEE

CoolBird
Publishing House
THE AUTHORS NEST

PART I
FEARFULLY &
WONDERFULY
MADE

Lesson 1
Old Shoes

As Mommy traced the outline of our feet (most often the older siblings), it was common to hear her say "take care of what you have" being that we were born in a poor family. She did this so that she could take the outline to the shoe store to buy our first pair of what we called, "Rock-n-rolls". "Won't get any more...", she'd continue to say. You remember...they were the black and white shoes that were impossible to destroy. The fact that they couldn't be destroyed meant that all the younger same-sex siblings could count on inheriting the prized shoes of the previous owner. It didn't matter much if we had the same shoe size because when the shoe finally came to you, it was just your time. You can imagine what this meant for me, having three older sisters. Ironically, the shoes were well preserved because my sisters took them off each day when they got home. I can still remember the laughs of the children at school as I wore the fourth-generation prize shoes.

When I became an adult and received a revelation, I realized that my parents were trying to teach us good stewardship. They knew that those shoes would have to sustain us through the many years to come. Not understanding what they were trying to teach, I longed for the day that my siblings would leave home and I'd be first. Not only first to wear new shoes, but also able to go with my parents to buy them and sometimes get my choice. Like many, I didn't understand that my sisters broke them in for me by having worn the shoes beforehand... I didn't have to go through the blisters on my feet as my older sister experienced from shoes being too tight. As a matter of fact, she became so good at breaking in shoes that she was called on by the neighbors to break in their new shoes! By the time shoes got to me, they'd been through enough wear that they should have brought me comfort rather than shame. Similarly, in a world filled with the glimmer of that which is new, the Christian, sometimes, feel ashamed of the same old Gospel. In an attempt to make all things new, we've tossed out the wisdom of those before us in exchange for the painful choices of what we thought to be new. Solomon, in his desire to know the fullness of existence tells us there's nothing new under the sun. What is, has been before.

"What has been will be again, what has been done will be done again; there is nothing new under the sun. Is there anything of which one can say, Look! This is something new? It was here already, long ago; it was here before our time." (Ecclesiastes 1:9-10 NIV)

In our attempt to save our children from what we thought was suffering, we've created a world spiraling out of control. (the spiraling should be related to children rather than the world). With the deception of something new, families no longer insist on following the carefully traced patterns of those before. God created the world to sustain man. He intended one generation to pass on its content to the next. Therefore, in essence, He said, "Take care of it, dress it, keep it, and have dominion over it …You won't get another." In chapter 2 of Genesis, we find God resting from all His work.

"Thus, the heavens and the earth were completed in all their vast array. By the seventh day God had finished the work he had been doing; so on the seventh day he rested from all his work. Then God blessed the seventh day and made it holy, because on it he rested from all the work

of creating that he had done." (Genesis 2:1-3 NIV)

He didn't rest in the sense of being tired, but rather in the sense of having completed His task. He rested from the need to add, to separate, and to set in place...even from the need to bless. All things were created and delivered to man so that He might start to operate in His God-given authority to rule and have dominion over all earthly creations. The first test of man's imagery of God was given as God brings all the animals and beast of the fields to see what Adam would call them, saying whatever you call them, that their names shall be.

"Now the LORD God had formed out of the ground all the wild animals and all the birds in the sky. He brought them to the man to see what he would name them; and whatever the man called each living creature, that was its name." (Genesis 2:19 NIV)

Man's assigning of names to all the creatures of the earth brought clarity of purpose and function to all things delivered into his hands. God could trust man because he was the manifested image of Himself in the earth. Man operated as God in the earth in that he had ultimate authority over all things created by God. Although he could not create, he had God's mind, bringing insight and understanding of purpose to all that was created.

Is it really all about us?

Lesson 2
Yes, It's All About Us

When I picked up the Word of God and realized that from Genesis to Revelation the Bible is all about us, my life exploded with such purpose. I gasp now at the thinking that enslaved me for years. The false humility I asserted as I found myself echoing, "It's not about me, it's about God." I found myself afraid to dream. I was too scared to want more than others for the fear of someone mistaking that I thought I was too good or ungrateful. Daddy drilled in our thinking as children that we should be grateful for what we had and not be high and mighty.

In an attempt to stay in my place (where I found myself never being), I tried to be content. Apostle Paul tells us that we can learn to be content. Paul didn't say this out of a place of settling for less, but rather out of a place of being complete in God. (This thought will be covered more in a later chapter.) Howbeit, Daddy meant well, and he knew, most likely, of all his children, I'd be the one to challenge him as I often did. He'd tell momma, "She's just hardheaded, Pauline!" If Daddy is looking down from heaven, he's probably saying, "See, I told you how she is..." But in total rebellion, I say out loud, "YES, IT'S ALL ABOUT US."

In His Holy Scriptures, I learned I am a part of God's plan even from the beginning. He had me and you in mind when He laid the foundation of the world. He was thinking of us from the time He called light out of darkness, creating day and night, until the time He created the beast and every creeping thing upon the earth. When I worked in public schools, the law required that teachers be certified in the content matter to teach students. Parents had to be informed if uncertified teachers were employed. Parents could request verification of each teacher's certification and, if not certified, could request the removal of the child to a certified teacher or school system with certified teachers.

To avoid the certification problem, most school systems adhered to the strict guidelines imposed by our state. As well, God imposes strict guidelines upon those teaching His Word. From the start of creation, we see the Master teacher adhering to His own strict standards. He reveals Himself as the Creator of all things and one of action. As He speaks, He makes, separates, sets in place, and blesses. He worked relentlessly calling forth first light. Then, with the same passion, we find the Creator, Master teacher over the next five days calling forth the remainder of creation. With full knowledge of what each created thing was and why it was being manifested, He graded each day's work by His own standards saying,

- The earth and the seas were good. (Genesis 1:10)
- The sun, moon, and stars to give light upon the earth were good. (Genesis 1:18)
- The abundant supply of fish of the sea and fowls of the air was good. (Genesis 1:21)
- The living creatures; cattle, beast of the field, creeping things to fill the earth were good. (Genesis 1:25)

All things were intentionally made and blessed with the potential to reproduce from its own kind. Creation would be the recipient of a world complete with all things we need to live and share in a wholesome relationship with God. Once God finished making everything that would inhabit the earth below and the heavens above, He conferred with every aspect of Himself (Father, Son, and Holy Spirit), allowing each to provide His own attribute,

- God, the Father who upholds the highest form of righteousness;
- God, the Son offering salvation, grace, and mercy (as man through free will and falls short of God's righteousness); and finally,
- God, the Spirit who empowers man to know the will of God, and to follow it.

The Godhead (Trinity) determined that man would be made in the image of the Godhead, blessed them and gave them dominion over all things upon the earth and within the seas. At the close of day six, the Master Teacher made the final assessment of His creation. Knowing that this was the completion of ALL things, He writes "It's very good."

"God saw all that he had made, and it was very good. And there was evening, and there was morning the sixth day." (Genesis 1:31 NIV)

So, how, then can we say it's not about us? Yes, it is all about us. The whole of creation was about you and me. We were in the mind of the Master from the foundations of the earth and will continue to be until His glorious return.

"For I know the plans I have for you, declares the LORD, plans to prosper you and not to harm you, plans to give you hope and a future." (Jeremiah 29:11 NIV)

28

Lesson 3
Light: The Real Source

All things start and end with God. When one attempts to determine life outside of this paradigm, he or she will spend life as in an endless cycle of starting over again and again. In the beginning, there were the heavens, earth, and waters. Focusing on the latter two, I'll refer to the earth as our outer self (the visible image we present to others) and the water as our soul the hidden, invisible self, the essence of who we are.

"In the beginning God created the heavens and the earth. The earth was without form, and void; and darkness was on the face of the deep. And the Spirit of God was hovering over the face of the waters. Then God said, "Let there be light"; and there was light." (Genesis 1:1-3 NKJV)

In the beginning, the earth was:

> All things start and end with God. Man may have excellent perceptions of life based on how things appear, but each must surmise- "Only God Knows."

- without form
- void
- and dark in appearance

In response to the earth's state of being, God moved, by His spirit, upon the waters. What God did literally to address the state of the earth, He desires to do with us today spiritually. Using our analogy of the earth representing the outer self and the waters representing the soul, in order for the visible image or the outside self to have form and light, we must allow God to move upon the invisible, hidden waters of our soul. Perhaps, the catastrophic and endless cycle continues because mankind fails to allow every aspect of their being to start and end with God. Therefore, it's essential to start where God starts, noticing the dark appearance of the exterior self. Then, allowing the Spirit to move upon the deeper waters of soul injuries and lifelong wounds.

Since the beginning of this discipleship class in 2012, I've supported many women through this process of identifying the discrepancy between the earth (outer self) and the waters (inner self). Each time I would start with the teaching and preaching of the earth (the disorder of the messed-up ways in which we order our lives and how this disorder affects everyone and everything around us). I spoke to the voids and the empty meaningless existence we often feel. I spoke to how we seek to fill our lives with relationships, chores, and events to avoid or deny the truth of what's present. I spoke to our darkness; the shame and guilt of things we wished had never happened, yet they did. I taught of the truth...many heard and were awakened to a need for change but could not actualize it no matter how many times they attended. Then, I taught about how often we made vows to change or to do better and potential barriers to that change. As I taught, I noticed more and more of my own earth and need for the Spirit to move upon my waters. I'd ask God, "Why do you allow me to keep teaching this when my own life is so messed up?" Seeing myself in some of them, I felt like a hypocrite. How could I know so much about the Master and suffer so much brokenness? Nothing about my life was well ordered. My relationship with my husband, children, and many others just hung in the balance. I woke up to disorder daily. I'm not talking about mounds of clutter packed in bags and boxes. I'm talking about the daily clutter of being surrounded with wrong thoughts, wrong people and the threat of making wrong choices. Yet, He kept calling me to teach, and they kept coming. One day after personally going through session 10, I had a revelation. Even God-fearing Christians can live in darkness forever if he or she doesn't allow God to move upon their waters, the deeper part of them. Everything starts in the soul realm. God works from the inside to manifest what He desires on the outside. The scriptures say that God, by His Spirit moved upon the waters. For all these years, you and I have been working on our earth and not allowing God to move upon the waters of our souls. I believe that we are in the time which the Prophet Isaiah speaks of, when gross darkness will cover the earth.

> Only God moves upon the dark areas of our existence bringing to light the essence of a truly changed life.

"Arise, shine, for your light has come, and the glory of the LORD rises upon you. See, darkness covers the earth and thick darkness is over the peoples, but the LORD rises upon you and his glory appears over you. Nations will come to your light, and kings to the brightness of your dawn.

"Lift up your eyes and look about you: All assemble and come to you; your sons come from afar, and your daughters are carried on the hip. Then you will look and be radiant, your heart will throb and swell with joy; the wealth on the seas will be brought to you, to you the riches of the nations will come." (Isaiah 60:1-5 NIV)

During this time, the light of God's glory will be manifested in the church as never before. In contrast to the dark sinful natures which we have labored to conceal, there will be the glory of God's Spirit lovingly covering the darkness. The Gentiles, those outside the faith, will be drawn as never before to the glory that belongs only to God. Mankind has sought to own God's glory. In response to this prideful pursuit, He reveals our true dark natures which have always existed and will forever exist. Even with our best attempt towards "good", we are still as filthy rags. When the Apostle Paul realizes the truth of his fleshly nature, he cries out to God to remove or correct it. Despite his persistence, the Master refuses his request, arguing that His grace was enough.

"Three times I pleaded with the Lord to take it away from me. But he said to me, "My grace is sufficient for you, for my power is made perfect in weakness." Therefore, I will boast all the more gladly about my weaknesses, so that Christ's power may rest on me."
(2 Corinthians 12:8-9 NIV)

Each time I stand to teach or preach I realize it's His amazing grace which allows me to stand. As long as we are on the earth, we will be a part of a world that was dark, void, and without form. Likewise, we will experience some form of darkness, formlessness, and void in this earthly existence. Nevertheless, we are the light of the world, despite our struggles. We are as the moon which only receives its light from the sun. Without the glory of God shining upon us, we all dwell in darkness. The spirit of the enemy has caused man to exalt himself above God and the heavens.

"How you are fallen from heaven, O Lucifer, son of the morning! How you are cut down to the ground, you who weakened the nations! For you have said in your heart: 'I will ascend into heaven, I will exalt my throne above the stars of God; I will also sit on the mount of the congregation on the farthest sides of the north; I will ascend above the heights of the clouds, I will be like the Most High." (Isaiah 14:12-14 NKJV)

Again, every aspect of our being must begin and end with God. If we seek to end the cycle of starting over, He must have His rightful place as Creator. Those who have enthroned themselves as God must be brought low in order to have a right relationship with Him. He tells Isaiah to tell the people, "I am the Lord and my glory will I not give to another."

"I am the LORD: that is my name: and my glory will I not give to another, neither my praise to graven images." (Isaiah 42:8 KJV)

Now, let's turn our attention more intently to a scriptural example of how God takes earth (outer self) and moves upon the waters (inner self) in a sustainable way. The Prophet Ezekiel's humility is on display as God's Spirit allows him to go into a valley of dry bones. There were many dry bones scattered about the valley's floor. Ezekiel walked around among the bones and was able to tell that the bones were dry throughout. After Ezekiel has examined the bones (the earth or outer self), God asks Ezekiel a question, "Can these bones again become living beings (Ezekiel 37:1-14 NIV)?" Examine Ezekiel's response before a sovereign God, as he answers, "Only you know." God then gives Ezekiel the message to preach to the bones. God's message is one of hope and restoration. He tells Ezekiel to tell them that He would make them have life again. He'd put flesh and muscles upon their bones and even cover them with skin (recreating the earth or outer self)! Finally, He'd breathe into their nostrils as He had at the beginning of creation (moved the waters or breathed into the inner self). As Ezekiel obeyed God's command to speak the Word, he saw the bones attaching, coming together as a full skeleton. Then, he saw muscles and flesh cover the bones. There was no breath. Anointed men and women of God can preach a Word that can cause broken lives and relationships to come together. Outwardly, it appears that people have gotten themselves together. Yet, it's hard to be consistent in their choices because there's no breath. There is nothing to sustain change due to the absence of the breath (the movement upon the soul or inner self), the Holy Spirit. God allowed Ezekiel to see the changed lives that resulted from the spoken Word! He then instructs Ezekiel to preach another message. He tells him to speak this time not to the bones, but to the winds. He tells him to call for the wind to come from the four corners of the earth and then breathes into the dead bodies so that they *all* may live.

When Ezekiel obeys God, he now sees breath come into the once dead bodies and they all live. Each stand upon their feet, an empowered army prepared to return to the place in God once abandoned. For a period, mankind has worked diligently to build lives from the outside. How glorious we have become in our elaborate temples. One generation has learned from the next how to present themselves for the best applause. While the crowds shout in grandeur, our soul cries in misery until the Master comes and breathe into our souls. Allow me to provide another example. King Saul was the people's choice for king. However, God removes Saul and appoints David to be king in his stead, calling him a man after His own heart.

"But now thy kingdom shall not continue: the LORD hath sought him a man after his own heart, and the LORD hath commanded him to be captain over his people, because thou hast not kept that which the LORD commanded thee." (1 Samuel 13:14 KJV)

David is not given this title because he was without flaws. His many flaws are seen throughout the scriptures. God refers to David in this manner because he learned the art of pleasing a God who was not impressed with his outward sacrifices. Many find comfort in the Psalms as we find King David lamenting over the condition of his soul.

Read his plea for cleansing and mercy:

"Have mercy on me, O God, according to your unfailing love; according to your great compassion blot out my transgressions. Wash away all my iniquity and cleanse me from my sin. For I know my transgressions, and my sin is always before me." (Psalms 51:1-3 NIV)

For over five years I've taught as commanded to the barren places in our lives. Hope came for restoration and renewal as we were able to love and forgive ourselves and others. Then, like Ezekiel, I hear God's call for me to summon the wind, the Holy Spirit, that He may speak to our souls, bringing truth in the inward parts. Let's travel back to the beginning to see what that breath created for us as man, then specifically as woman in order to return to our original design and source.

Lesson 4
Woman: Her Beginning

Having made everything He desired to make and being assured that mankind was sustained and without lack, God made man "in His own image" (Genesis 1:27 NIV). When man was created, God addressed all his needs for living including a communal relationship with Him. God gave him dominion or authority over all His creation and put him in the garden to dress it and keep it. However, God did limit man's authority. He could eat freely of every tree in the garden except the tree of the knowledge of good and evil. God tells him that he would surely die should he eat of this tree. This death might suggest a relational separation from God and the removal of man's God-given authority. Then, *"The LORD God said, "It is not good for the man to be alone. I will make a helper suitable for him."* (Genesis 2:18 NIV) Interestingly, God went back to creating beasts of the field and birds of the air and brought them to Adam to name and subdue in the authority God gave him (v. 19, 20). When God prepares to make woman, He puts man into a deep sleep, a state of inactivity, and crafts the woman from man's rib. Using Himself as the highest standard, He graded man and woman saying, not "good," but rather, "very good."

Let's explore this more. Was there something missing in the man that he needed the woman? Did God make a mistake in leaving something out of man that He needed to create woman? Absolutely not! The Apostle Peter assures us that there is never any insufficiency in God.

"According as his divine power hath given unto us all things that pertain

36

unto life and godliness, through the knowledge of him that hath called us to glory and virtue." (2 Peter 1:3 KJV)

Mankind can be perpetually assured that we have all things needed to glorify God in every aspect of life. The woman is not an after-thought where God says, "I forgot to do something." God had already determined what man (humans) would need to fulfill His acceptable stand. What would He do about it? He'd make man a helper. We understand that this helper is the woman.

I asked:

- Why didn't God just make the woman and put her in the garden as He did the man?
- What's in this time lapse?
- Why didn't God just speak as He did in other instances just as He called forth all of heaven and earth?

He spoke a whole world into being. What's in this coming forth of woman? What's the purpose of God's intentional delay? When something is made it has all the elements of being identified in and of itself. When God presents the woman to the man, he sees woman in her fullness. She had everything needed for life and her Godly purpose. Every woman must know that she is complete in God. She is not just "made", but fearfully and wonderfully made. (Psalm 139:14-16, NIV) "Marvelous are the works of God!" I know that very well, and it should be our response to every questionable context of our existence. Even before He fashioned you in your mother's womb, He had a plan for our lives. Woman is not an after-thought. I believe woman was in the mind of God even while He was waiting to bring light into a whole world that laid in darkness (all was in His mind before He spoke or created, thus already in existence). I believe God was intentional in how and when He crafted her. Perhaps. He wanted her to have everything she needed before she came to life. Perhaps, He waited until Adam awakened in his own consciousness of needing a companion suitable for him as he looked at the pairing of the other created things. Perhaps, He steps back and considers the whole of His plan or vision for earth and man, then concludes she's the second needful being to make it happen.

Though we might theorize, we can't know for sure the answers to those questions. I believe God kept the woman hidden away until the man became aware of a need within himself that nothing else in the earth could satisfy. God puts him to sleep affirming that man had no direct involvement in how woman was formed. Nevertheless, we do know they were both created at and by the Hand of God as equals; equally complete for each other, yet with different responsibilities and functions.

Lesson 5
Man's Deep Sleep

As soon as man recognizes that something is missing, God puts him to sleep. Although man is made in the image of God, he is not God. Therefore, he can never be called our creator. Although man was made in God's image and even given limited authority, God draws the line between fleshly man and the divine. When God prepares to make woman, He puts man into a deep sleep, a state of inactivity. When mankind moves beyond his established authority, God puts him to sleep, causing him to acknowledge his personal limitations. The lines of distinctions must always be clear. God calls mankind to live righteously and upright. Man will never in a fleshly body, achieve a state of total authority. We find this need for clarity as Satan's attention is directed towards Job.

"In the land of Uz there lived a man whose name was Job. This man was blameless and upright; he feared God and shunned evil. He had seven sons and three daughters, and he owned seven thousand sheep, three thousand camels, five hundred yoke of oxen and five hundred donkeys, and had many servants. He was the greatest man among all the people of the East. His sons used to hold feasts in their homes on their birthdays, and they would invite their three sisters to eat and drink with them.

When a period of feasting had run its course, Job would make arrangements for them to be purified. Early in the morning he would sacrifice a burnt offering for each of them, thinking, "Perhaps my children have sinned and cursed God in their hearts. This was Job's regular custom. One day the angels came to present themselves before the LORD, and Satan also came with them. The LORD said to Satan, "Where have you come from?" Satan answered the LORD, "From roaming throughout the earth, going back and forth on it. Then the

LORD said to Satan, have you considered my servant Job? There is no one on earth like him; he is blameless and upright, a man who fears God and shuns evil." (Job 1:1-8 NIV)

Look how God refers to Job's uprightness. He applauds his reverence for Him, detesting all evil. Why does God purposefully allow Satan to bring Job to seemingly demise, then? Could the answer possibly be man's inability to handle earthly possessions whether they be natural or spiritual without a sense of being God's equal? Not only have others taken notice of Job's Godly postulation, so had Satan. When God refers to Job, Satan allows Him to know that he's seen him during his continual strolls up and down…to and fro in the earth. However, he knows he can not touch Job unless the hedge of protection is moved from around him. God removes the hedge giving Satan the opportunity to move against Job's earth.

Chapter after chapter you find Job wallowing in the ashes of his earthly deplore. Well intended friends came to assist Job as he sifts through his ruins. God allows each man to postulate a probable cause for Job's demise, as Job attempts to defend his righteous innocence. Finally, as if God has had enough of their words, He speaks in a whirlwind of fury, asking Job about his part in creation.

"Then the LORD spoke to Job out of the storm. He said: "Who is this that obscures my plans with words without knowledge? Brace yourself like a man; I will question you, and you shall answer me. "Where were you when I laid the earth's foundation? Tell me, if you understand." (Job 38:1-4 NIV)

God allows Job to know that though he had earthly

possessions and even diligently pursued righteousness, he was not involved in creation...its darkness, voids, or formlessness. God continues His rebuke of Job through chapter 41, bringing Job to ultimate humility. However, it's not until chapter 42, that we find Job breaking in humble repentance.

"Then Job replied to the LORD: I know that you can do all things; no purpose of yours can be thwarted. You asked, who is this that obscures my plans without knowledge? Surely, I spoke of things I did not understand, things too wonderful for me to know. You said, listen now, and I will speak; I will question you, and you shall answer me. My ears had heard of you but now my eyes have seen you.

> It's not our right behaving that warrants a goodly life but a right heart. Often times, we learn this through calamity.

Therefore, I despise myself and repent in dust and ashes." (Job 42:1-6 NIV)

It's here that Job's consciousness is awakened to the knowledge of God. He, like many of us, had spoken of God as learned through words. We preach, teach, even sing lyrics of a God we know not. Through Job's suffering he had come to see God in His fullness. He then feared and reverenced His dominance over all creation. Mankind will continue to speak of a God whom he or she knows not until each is brought low in reverence of Him.

"The fear of the LORD is the beginning of wisdom, and knowledge of the Holy One is understanding." (Proverbs 9:10 NIV)

I do believe that God is awakening dominion men, those who will take authority in a dark and broken world. While many are asleep and unaware of his destiny in God, he will soon awake to the woman God is preparing. This woman of God will win the heart of a Godly man who recognizes her as what he needs to make him a powerful kingdom man.

Lesson 6
Woman: Her Purpose & Identity I

"Sugar and spice and everything nice that what little girls are made of" …

This little phrase made girls of my childhood day giggle. Now of course, boys were made of snails and puppy dog tails. The description wasn't meant to be taken literally but was intended to establish differences in the character traits of boys and girls. Yet, I wonder if exposure to this nursery rhyme would have made a difference in how our young millennials understand or see themselves or each other. In my countless hours of counseling sessions with young elementary school girls, I heard problems unimaginable to me when I was their age. Their experiences were certainly not the sugar and spice that we giggled about as little girls!

I dare not attempt to tell you what you're made of, but how I long to tell you what you were made for! Anytime the purpose of something is not known, the result will be abuse inevitably. If we use Merriam-Webster's definition of abuse as improper use or treatment, it's clear to see how not knowing the purpose of something, whether a person or thing, can lead to improper use. Nevertheless, the severity of that improper use or treatment is directly associated with the degree of impact that person or thing experiences. For years I suffered emotional abuse in part by others and in part self-inflicted. Because I wasn't aware of my image and likeness in God, I succumbed to those early messages that I wasn't good enough or not as valuable as others. In adulthood, I built upon those messages and created new ones for myself. After

20 years of responding to life out of those messages, one day I stopped on the side of the road in Birmingham, Alabama. I was so tired of whatever, and I screamed out to God, "If you are real, then tell me who I am". "Why did you create me?" "If this is all there is, then I don't want to live another day"! It was that Saturday that God called me by name. I started living a life that I hoped would bring Him honor. I'm not saying that I still didn't error from time to time, but I can tell you that I started to live life with purpose. Being made was a difficult concept for me because seemingly nothing was ever complete. As a child, there was always something needing to be done first. Oh, how I hated the word "*then*" because it always preceded permission being granted for whatever request I made, no matter how seemingly minute.

- Eat vegetables, then have ice cream;
- Sweep the floor, then play outside;
- Wash dishes, then watch television;
- Say prayers; then go to bed.

Seemingly, there were prerequisites to everything. I rarely remember a time when "then" was "now." Perhaps, it's out of this sense of "nothing ever being complete" that I struggled with being made. For years I struggled with my image. A dark-skinned, nappy-headed female growing up in a world where lighter, fair complexion women with "good hair" (the term used for hair that was straighter and naturally wavy) were called beautiful. I survived the agony of bleaching creams which left the body various shades of whatever color and burnt necks and ears from hot straightening combs...And not to mention the loss of hair resulting from improper relaxing. Somehow, I thought that if

44

I worked hard enough at changing my image, then I'd feel good about whatever I was feeling bad about or being told that I should feel bad about. Without knowing who started the whole idea of who was and wasn't beautiful, I bought into the idea and decided that I didn't have enough going for me to make the line-up. My sister was really pretty growing up. She was popular and it was confirmed that she was a beauty especially when she won Homecoming queen her senior year. Although I wasn't pretty like my sister, I tried to walk in her footsteps. I won the Homecoming queen my senior year too. Surely then I'd feel this sense of being made. My feelings were quite the opposite. I felt that everyone looked at me and wondered how I'd won...Especially since the queen before me was so beautiful. Seeing that I didn't qualify for the hall of beauty, I was glad that the local news didn't take too many pictures for the paper. A few people congratulated me, but for the most part, I didn't talk about it. I didn't even know there were pictures at home until I stumbled across one in my sister's photo album. I never returned to crown my successor the following year. The dress I'd determined to wear wasn't ready. Daddy fussed about the cost of getting me to and from college for this one event which further supported that it had all been one big mistake.

Since I didn't feel pretty, I tried to compensate for what was lacking in other ways. I wanted people to like me so often times I'd put their needs and desires before my own. By the time I was in my mid-twenties I was drowning in so much debt I considered filing for bankruptcy. When I considered how I'd gotten there, I realized it was the purchase of relationships. I thought having people around would make me popular like my sister. I paid a high price and had nothing to show for it. As I struggled to rise from my deplorable state, I found none in the crowd to assist. The crowd slowly drifted away as I stopped picking up the tab at dinner or throwing the party at my place. I found myself like those who were always trying to get on their feet... "Just help me out this time, I'll give it back when such and such comes through". This is what I'd promise. I found myself needing to beg in a land of plenty.

I'd often turn to my family for help. I believed myself to be a burden, especially when I couldn't explain why I was working and still needing so much help. My Big Daddy (affectionate name given to grandfathers in the South) warned the family to cut me off before they all end up in the same condition as me. Apparently, he was the voice of authority because one by one I found them refusing to help me. Big Daddy said I was ruining the family name that he'd worked so hard to build. When I'd come into the front yard, I mean before I could even walk across the planked porch or even knock on the door, he'd yell, "Get away from here you sorry devil!"

I stopped running from the creditors and took my car and turned it in. I'm not sure when it happened, but I knew I'd changed. Big Daddy must have known too because I was able to come in the house. I didn't ask for money anymore and if I did, I was sure to give it back at the time I promised. I was becoming a woman of integrity. I was spending more time with Big Daddy and learning much about being thrifty and resourceful. By now, Daddy was dead, but he made sure that he told me about Daddy's vices and why he wasn't more successful. I thought Big Daddy was a hard man. He was "stingy" (thrifty) even with his tears. He told me proudly,

"When your Daddy (his son) died, I only dropped two tears and that's it girl." I suppose he wasn't going to spend a lifetime crying about things he couldn't change. I saw life from two extremes- a place of being too easy or overly compassionate and a place of being too hard with two tears. What I really found out was that both foundational thoughts were from a place of fear. Later, I discovered my foundational thoughts were fear based. I gave to others because I feared rejection. Big Daddy withheld giving out of fear of losing. When God receives us as His own, He teaches us that everything we do must be from a place of perfected love. Whether your ways are described as too easy or too hard, the truth is that it must be done in love. In perfected love, there is no torment.

"There is no fear in love; but perfect love casts out fear, because fear involves torment. But he who fears has not been made perfect in love." (I John 4:18 NKJV)

The Prophet Jeremiah conveys the plight of one's heart as he describes it as deceitful and desperately wicked (Jeremiah 17:9 NIV). Ultimately, the prophet contends that no one can truly know the heart. King David agrees with Jeremiah's evaluation of the heart's deceptive nature. However, he doesn't settle with the idea of it being beyond exposure or cure. The King knows that God is the creator of all things and that nothing is hidden from him, not even the contents of the heart (Psalm 139:1-7 NIV). As King David, we must allow God to search the heart, try the spirit, and reveal the motive behind each deed (Psalm 139:23-24 KJV). It's only then that we discover that place of ultimate truth. Moreover, it is only after discovering the truth that we can be empowered to return to our original design of seeing ourselves as God formed us- in His image and likeness.

I thought I wanted to be like my sister, my Big Daddy and many others I'd encountered as I sought to be made in His image. The more truth I embraced, the more I became free. The more I asked God to search and know my heart, the clearer the motives became behind my acts of kindness and the clearer my identity became. I longed to be re-shaped into the image of God. As women taken from the rib of man, fully and solely made by the hand and breath of God, you must know that you are perfect and entire and needing nothing outside of God to affirm your purpose (design), identity, worth, and the purpose for your life's call in the earth. Divine women let us call forth the wind which is the breath of God to breathe life into our slain souls so that we may live!

"Then said he unto me, Prophesy unto the wind, prophesy, son of man, and say to the wind, Thus saith the Lord GOD; Come from the four winds, O breath, and breathe upon these slain, that they may live." (Ezekiel 37:9 KJV)

Lesson 7
Woman: Her Purpose & Identity II

If you have lived or are possibly still living an abused life as I did, it's not too late to change your life. Maybe you see your daughter on the same path towards abuse as you have lived. I tell you, it's not too late. It's not too late to say, "Baby you were made for more than the abuse you are suffering." The Prophet Hosea (4:6 NKJV) says, *"My people are destroyed for lack of knowledge. Because you have rejected knowledge... Because you have forgotten the law of your God..."*

It was not that knowledge wasn't available in Hosea's day or in our day, but the problem is that the knowledge is being rejected. I have the opportunity to speak in women conferences and during the meet and greet, I hear women say, "I'm Sally Doe, married to Jack Doe and we have two lovely Doe children." She continues, "I am a secretary at Doe Enterprise, I graduated from Doe University, and attend Doe Assembly of God where my husband is..." The audience claps and Sally Doe takes her seat. Just glad to be a Doe at heart. My heart sinks to think that perhaps, she doesn't know who *she* is. Yes, she's a wife, mother, career woman, church member, but that's not who she is. Yes, God has allowed her to operate in these various offerings to bring Him glory, but that's not who she is. Everything God created, whether living or non-living was intentional and purposeful. God never started the creation of something new until what He previously created was able to sustain what He was about to make and meet His standard of "good."

Although I don't look like what I did when I was twenty, I'm

49

still God's masterpiece. Some things you and I will never be able to do again. You'll never look that way again, stop staring at the photos. Let it go! Stop being impressed at the people who say you don't look your age. You might not look that age, and that's good. Keep them guessing. However, you, God, and a few other folk know your age. Be thankful for all things and bring Him the Honor He deserves at every season of your life.

When a car manufacturer makes an automobile, they are given the right to put their emblem or logo on it. This symbol gives them full rights to the craftsmanship and warranties of the vehicle. In the same way, God has full rights to the details and crafting of you. Everything that makes you who you are is established in the mind and plan of God. Although many are called woman, there's only one you. You are the original plan of God being manifested in the earth, in the exact time and place you're in.

The man was placed in the garden first. He was allowed to experience dominion and authority in the garden...naming things and calling into being the things created. A man who knows and operates in the authority of God in the earth is essential. Man's lack of knowledge in this area is likely the reason for so much chaos in the world. God permitted Adam to name His created being. Adam said, "She shall be called woman because she was taken out of man" (Genesis 2:23 KJV). I believe in this statement Adam recognized her as God's declaration of being a needful part of him. Woman was made intentionally from man and for him (1 Corinthians 11:8-9) and the man recognized her worth and value. Man has the authority to name what God has created, but he doesn't have the authority to create. Man is flesh and spirit; God is spirit only. If man created, quite likely he would resort to flesh to determine what he needs. Thus, it's important that a woman knows her worth and value in the earth as well. She must understand that her relationship with man enhances his ability to call order in the earth. To do this, she must see herself as complete in God. She must never feel the need for something or someone to make her feel complete or more equipped for the mission. God has given the woman everything she will ever need to live on the earth. Who is this rare find that the writer of Proverbs refers to as priceless?

"Who can find a virtuous woman? for her price is far above rubies." (*Proverbs 31:10 KJV*)

This is the woman of God who brings honor to not only her husband, but her entire household. The Bible says her husband is honored in the gates and that she provides for the household. Even if she makes more than the husband, she uses her earnings to bless rather than manipulate. She makes sure her family is well dressed and provided for... Not only does she take care of her house, she gives to others in need. She doesn't have time for idleness and gossiping with girlfriends. Her husband calls her blessed and her children honor her too. I thank God that my husband has trust in me and knows that no matter his weaknesses, I'll do him good and never evil, all the days of his life. Even if my husband came today and said I have someone else, or he feels the need to move on, I'll still pray for him that he never ceases from being the kingdom man he was created to be. I know that what a person does is not who they are. My prayer for my family is always, "Lord cause them to be what you created them to be". My son works as an engineer. This was a goal of his for a long time. I pray that he doesn't get lost in his career and forgets God. Should he lose his way, my prayer is that he soon comes to himself, realize that he was created to subdue the earth and bring God glory. The Prophet Isaiah prophesied of our day saying, seven women will grab hold of one man saying we will eat our own bread, wear our own clothes, just take away our shame by giving us your name.

"In that day seven women will take hold of one man and say, we will eat our own food and provide our own clothes; only let us be called by your name. Take away our disgrace!" (Isaiah 4:1 NIV)

When a woman has no sense of identity or purpose in God, you may find her doing things like working all day while the man she thinks is hers is riding other women around in her car. This isn't something she protests, as long as he gives her his name (tells her who she is by association). He can be mine on Monday and yours on Tuesday. She sadly convinces herself that she'd rather have a piece of man than to have no man at all. What she fails to realize is that she's better being alone with God than to have a man that is asleep to who she is, or more importantly, who doesn't know who he was created to be in the earth. If you are a single Kingdom woman your attention should be on bringing God honor in every area of your life. You don't have time to be in the drama of "baby daddy" and "my man." Get off social media fussing about a man who doesn't have a clue about who you were created to be!

A woman complete in God causes man to take notice of her, not by what she is wearing or not wearing. Billions of dollars are spent by women desiring to alter their earthly presentation. The Apostle Peter urges women to not allow her beauty to be only of an outward show but rather of an inward assurance which speaks of her wholeness in God.

> God did not make man until He made everything on the earth. Therefore, mankind has everything needed to live a Godly and purposeful life.

"Your beauty should not come from outward adornment, such as elaborate hairstyles and the wearing of gold jewelry or fine clothes. Rather, it should be that of your inner self, the unfading beauty of a gentle and quiet spirit, which is of great worth in God's sight."
(1 Peter 3:3 NIV)

In Genesis, the woman complete in God was deceived of Satan to take from something of the earth to be wise or better. The Bible says that when she gave to the man, he did eat, and their eyes were both opened to see nakedness (faults), marring their relationship with not only God, but with each other. Don't allow the deceptions of beauty, wealth, acceptance, or someone else's identity entice you into taking something from the earth realm that has no way of living up to its advertisement. You are already complete but the only way you'll realize your true beauty, wealth, and acceptance is to be found in Him. I deal with this subject more in depth in Part II.

Lesson 8
Woman's Value: Who's Grading Your Paper?

My son said to me one day when he was in high school, "Mom, most of my friends say you're nice." I wanted to ask additional questions as to how they came to that conclusion. Questions like, "What standard did they use to call me nice opposed to someone they referred to as not nice?" Rather than query my son further, I decided I'd let it end at that. I learned to be careful about the evaluations of others. A lesson I learned without knowing that it was a lesson, until much later.

When I was in elementary school, there were certain teachers who would avoid the drudgery of grading papers by allowing the students to exchange papers after an examination. Each student would grade the paper of their neighbor adjacent to them. Perhaps, my classmates didn't understand the term neighbor. Each time I tried to give my paper to a student on either side, in front or back of me he or she would say, "I have a paper." It was bad enough that I struggled to spell, forgetting whether the "r" went before or after the "u" in February. Then, to feel personally rejected by my neighbors was so overwhelming that I dreaded Fridays. I'd pretend to be sick each week to avoid going to school. Daddy finally decided that it was no way I was sick every Friday, so he made me go anyway.

Every Friday I'd run from student to student trying to get someone to take my paper. The teacher would make someone finally take it while at the same time the kids were protesting that they had one already. Remember, I was a poor speller and usually didn't do well on the test. By recess, the children were calling me "dummy, dummy." Fridays became so tormenting that as soon as the test was over, I'd start sniffing. The teacher would say, "What's wrong with you, McKinney (my maiden name)? Every week you start that crying, just bring that paper here." It wasn't that I had become a better speller, but I found out that the teacher had the power that students didn't have. Rather than marking all the months wrong because I forgot to capitalize them, she called me to her desk, or wrote in big red letters, "Don't forget to capitalize." I found out that the students didn't take my paper because they disliked me, but because they'd given their paper to a friend who didn't mark words wrong, or who'd make the needed corrections without the teacher knowing. Perhaps she knew but didn't think it was important enough to challenge.

Even in elementary school God was teaching me a valuable lesson. The students could grade your paper, but only the teacher could decide if you were promoted or retained. I mistakenly feared the students, who didn't have the power to say, "Don't forget to capitalize" or "You can take the test over Monday because you need a little more practice" as the teacher sometimes did. I even found out that the teacher could promote you to the next grade on "condition!" She did my brother that way when he'd miss a lot of school during the harvest season. Daddy would keep him home to work the fields. "Condition" is what I call God's mercy. He's so merciful to us that He's willing to give us the opportunity to do it again and again. The righteous fall many times, but he delivers him from them all (Psalm 34:19).

When my son said, "My friends say you're nice..." it didn't mean as much because I learned years earlier to give my paper to the teacher. I learned that giving my paper to the teacher prevented the students from evaluating me, but it also prevented me from cheating the times she said, "I'm going to let you grade your own papers." In addition to grading my competency, the test graded my integrity of heart. How tempted I was to cheat! I rarely did because I was so afraid of the teacher. What if she could tell I changed the answer? What if she graded it over rather than taking my word for it?

Now, when I sense that someone has my paper, I quickly get it and give it to the Teacher. The one who's always full of mercy and has an awesome plan for my life despite my flaws and weaknesses. I suppose I never thought I was "made" in the image of God because there was always something wrong according to someone else's grading. How grateful I am to sit in life's classrooms and no longer fear the students! Now, I have full confidence in the Master Teacher whose plan for my life includes an expected end but mercy and grace along the way toward that end. Being made in the image of God doesn't mean that we don't have flaws, it means that we are able to see each other as the Teacher sees us...with unconditional love.

Lesson 9
He Called Her Woman

So far, we've examined six days of God's handiwork in creating the light, moon, stars in the sky, water, plants, and animals in the earth. He created man to have dominion over all those things. We have determined that God noted that Adam needed a helper suitable for him. God did not just speak her into existence, as He did the sun, moon fowls, fish, beast and every other part of His creation, He took her from Adam. Both man and his helper, like the other creations were complete in and of themselves. Before man is given the task of naming woman, God examines his ability to name his lesser creatures. He brought every beast of the field and every fowl of the air to Adam to see what he would call them. Any name man assigned to them would be their names perpetually. It appears that such a task would be exhausting. We find man prescribing names to the cattle, the fowls of the air, and every beast of the field. I do not think that the process was as exhausting as it appears. Since God doesn't regard time like man, I suggest that God, unlike man, did not line up the creatures one by one and have the man assign them names. I believe it was a gradual process and over a period of time.

As man encountered various creatures and noted that one differed from another, he assigned classifying names to each. Thus, God puts man to sleep and takes out of him the only thing he needs to create woman, his rib. He then closes the flesh thereby, closing all aspects of man's physical involvement in the creation of the woman.

"So, the LORD God caused the man to fall into a deep sleep; and while he was sleeping, he took one of the man's ribs and then closed up the place with flesh. Then the LORD God made a woman from the rib he had taken out of the man, and he brought her to the man." (Genesis 2:21-22 NIV)

Man only recognizes and names what God has created or made. God had no problem with trusting man with this task because He knew that man was in His image before the fall. He was directed by His Spirit and saw all things through His perceptions. One seeking to buy a car generally approaches the dealer with basic knowledge of what should be present before a car can be deemed a car. It's doubtful that this person would settle for a steering wheel, tires, a few car parts, and say, "I'll take this one and add a few things." No, this person not only insists that all parts be present, but that each meet the standard ascribed to its name. He or she also asks that the dealer provides the accompanying manual so that the car will always perform at optimal performance. The manual provides knowledge of its parts, repair needs, and service requirements.

The first man recognized the woman because she was complete having everything working together as God prescribed. In response to God's finished work, man assigned her the name… "Woman". Man knew not only who she was, but that she was a part of him.

"The man said, her bones have come from my bones. Her body has come from my body. She will be named woman, because she was taken out of a man." (Genesis 2:23 NIV)

He knew assuredly that she was the missing part that he longed for and that she would also be his helper in subduing the earth. He recognized her completeness as a part of himself. She was complete and he was complete, but He recognized that she was a part of him. In their completeness, they partner to accomplish the tasks

> Kingdom Man will recognize Kingdom Woman.

and plan God had for their creation, yet each has a separate function but being of one another. Nothing missing or lacking in either, but the wholeness compliments each other's being so much that it's advantageous for them to "marry" themselves for a fuller existence. He recognized that she is him (equal in creation and value or worth), having a different function (authority or responsibility). Kingdom man will recognize Kingdom woman. He doesn't see her as something or someone he needs to work on to meet his physical whims. He recognizes her as God's workmanship. If there are problems, he refers to the manual, the Bible. He seeks the mind of the manufacturer, God, so that she performs at her optimal performance concerning the works of her hands. A woman complete in God causes a man to take notice of her.

Lesson 10
What is Your Name?

There's much in a name; the Bible speaks of the value in a good name.

"A good name is more desirable than great riches."
(Proverbs 22:1 NIV)

Since many people can be called by the same name, at times it is necessary to include other identifying characteristics, such as "The Joe who just moved to town", or "Who is the brother of Sharon, the one who joined our church last fall." If that doesn't land the name, other identifiers follow, "You know, he's tall and skinny, kind-a cute...He was at the mall with Lynn last weekend." Perhaps, it's the "They say he has a baby by Shaun..." part that is mentioned before you finally hear, "Oh yeah, I know who you're talking about, but I didn't know he was Shaun's baby daddy." With an exhaustive list of information to clarify who's who, far more information than needed or asked is provided that may or may not indicate that person's identity. How careless we have been to assign one's identity based on a list of outward characteristics, possible deeds, or acquaintances.

Yes, there's much in a name. When I worked as a counselor in public school, I recount the numerous times children sat crying in my office because of some demeaning name he or she was called on the playground, on the way to the bus, or at the lunch table. Hearing the "at times" physical and descriptive name which caused the devastating blow, I'd drop my head trying not to take note of the area in question, and to conceal the facial expressions of my thoughts that whoever

60

said it called that just about right. In my struggle not to laugh, I inevitably asked each kid the same question:

"What is your name?" As I tried to understand, He or she would say their name. Then I'd ask them, "Is (what ever name they were called) your name?" Muffled behind sobs, I'd hear the same response, "No." Then I'd ask, "Why did you respond if that was not your name?"

Years have passed since I left my little office in the school. Yet, they still come. They're no longer little boys or girls but rather grown men and women fighting back the sobs of lost or broken identities. They carry with them painful memories of deeds but more often words spoken by parents, friends, mates, or even out of

> Personal identity is essential not only in this world but also in eternity.

their own souls. Jacob, too, had this inward struggle as God changes his name to Israel (Genesis 35:10 KJV). Perhaps the struggle started in the womb as he and his brother Esau fought (Genesis 25:22-23 KJV). When Rebekah asked the reason for the struggle, God informed her that there were two nations in her womb and the elder will serve the younger. Before Jacob was brought to his mother and father to be named, God knew who he was to be in the womb. Perhaps, finally coming to a place where he could no longer resist what God created him for, as an adult, Jacob separated himself from everyone and everything he labored so hard to achieve. As he struggled through the darkness of night, he faced his real identity in God's question, "What is your name?" He replied from the only awareness he'd ever known, "I am Jacob." No longer can you be Jacob; you must now be called

61

Israel. You will give birth to nations.

"And he arose that night and took his two wives, his two female servants, and his eleven sons, and crossed over the ford of Jabbok. He took them, sent them over the brook, and sent over what he had. Then Jacob was left alone; and a Man wrestled with him until the breaking of day. Now when He saw that He did not prevail against him, He touched the socket of his hip; and the socket of Jacob's hip was out of joint as He wrestled with him. And He said, Let Me go, for the day breaks. But he said, I will not let You go unless You bless me! So, He said to him, what is your name? He said, Jacob. And He said, your name shall no longer be called Jacob, but Israel; for you have struggled with God and with men and have prevailed." (Genesis 32:22-28 NKJV)

In the Word while God was preparing to do astounding work through His man or woman, He often changed their names…

- Abram became Abraham
- Sarai became Sarah
- Saul became Paul
- Simon became Peter

Until you and I refuse to answer to the names assigned to us in the earth by those having no knowledge of our identity, we will forever long to be in His image. My dear sister, I long to meet you. What's your name? Join me as we discover our true identity in God. How sad it will be in that day, as we seek to enter the Kingdom, that we hear the dreaded words, "I know not your name."

PART I

LESSON REVIEW

LIFE CHANGING TRUTHS

- All things start and end with God. He is the Alpha and the Omega. Man may have excellent perceptions of life based on how things appear, but like the Prophet Ezekiel, each must surmise- "Only God Knows."

- Only God moves upon the dark areas of our existence bringing to light the essence of a truly changed life. Anointed men and women of God can preach a Word which can cause broken lives, even relationships to come together. But ultimately, only God through the Holy Spirit can cultivate changed lives.

- All things were made by God with a specific purpose in mind. All things were made and blessed with the potential to reproduce and sustain itself.

- Of All things created, Man and Woman are God's Masterpieces, created to show forth His image in the earth. Everything made was made with man and woman in mind. All things made were made in response to mankind's call to represent the image of God in the earth.

- Mankind has been equipped with everything needed to bring God glory. God did not make man until He had made everything on the earth. Therefore, mankind has everything needed to live a Godly and purposeful life.

- God gave man limited authority over creation. Man exercised his God-given authority as he subdued and brought living things under his control. This was first noticed in his assigning names to every living thing.

- Woman is manifested to man when he acknowledges

64

his need for that which he cannot satisfy. A woman who is confident in her identity in God will cause men to take notice of her.

- It's of vital importance that you know your name. Personal identity is essential not only in this world but also in eternity.

PART II
BROKEN IMAGES

INTRODUCTION

Shattered Pieces...

Of a truth, it was an accident...And without a doubt, it was my fault! Although part of me wanted to ask, "Why would you put such a prized possession on the coffee table anyway?" I'm talking about the would've been heirloom vase Mommy purchased by saving the green stamps she'd get each time she went to the grocery store. I knew it was priceless. Mommy had circled it in the catalog along with the other possible items she'd allow us to get if we were *good*. I remember the long-awaited day... mom had enough stamps for the vase. I remember her reaching into the loft pulling down the shoe box holding the stacks of books. Seemingly, there were hundreds of them. She counted them...one, two, three...I saw the rarely seen contour of a smile brush gently across her face. Mommy carefully put rubber bands around the books of stamps before she sent them off. The vase finally arrived, and Mommy put it in the living room. You remember the one particular room in the house that we kept clean. To my knowledge, everyone in the neighborhood had the same things in their living room (that particular room) ...a couch, chair, coffee table, two end tables, pictures of Dr. King, President Kennedy, and Jesus in the center. Now, Mommy would surely be the neighbors' envy with this priceless vase added to her living room's décor.

Considering the importance of the living room itself, every child knew the two rules of the living room – don't play in it and don't mess it up. In fact, I can't ever remember sitting in the living room for any length of time. When grown folk came to the house we were sent away. No one really said to go, we knew the look that meant to leave after we'd made whatever polite greeting we could muster up, and after we'd been counted and correctly identified...

"Pauline, which one is this?" So, surely, there was no reason for Mommy to rehearse the living room rules to us after she added the vase; however, she did indeed! This priceless vase wasn't just a nice piece to this enshrined room but a status symbol; we were a level above our neighbors. In case anyone was uncertain of the pricelessness of the vase, one only had to look at its gold rim circling the top and oriental print on both sides and recall it had taken all but a few of Mommy's green stamps! I knew this. Before I go on and you decide to cast an unfair verdict, remember I did say it was an accident! No one intentionally disobeys, they just do somehow. Well... it happened. Despite Mommy's review of the living room's rules, I accidentally ran through the living room- not watching and the vase tipped over and hit the wood floor. It was broken...But not in such a manner that shattered pieces lie over the floor, but large and distinct pieces that with careful manipulation and some super glue, it could be put back together. At least it could be put together enough to deceive those who may never find the need to examine it any closer than what it was meant to be... for show (or to impress). I did find some glue. Though it wasn't super glue, it did the job of holding it together enough to deceive the onlookers.

I remember how afraid I was of someone finding out though. Questions crowded my mind...What would happen to me? What would happen to our family if someone saw the concealed crack down the center of the vase? Certainly, we'd lose our status in the community and be found imposters. Would I ever see the rarely seen smile sweep across Mommy's face again? I can't recall exactly the outcome of the vase. Perhaps, something so traumatic happened that I pushed it into my subconscious. However, I do recall the misery associated with the cover-up. How many people live shattered, broken lives day after day with the worries of someone finding out or learning their secret? How many of you reading have lived in misery and anguish, condemning yourself because you heard the rules, you knew not to do it, and you walked right into it anyway? Even if you managed to put the broken pieces together as best you can, you live in fear of someone possibly noticing the visible cracks. Thus, you isolate yourself from the close stares that come with close relationships.

My friend, may you find freedom in the pages that follow. Know of truth, that we are all marred and broken vessels in the hand of the potter, God. Only He can smooth out the rough edges and mend the broken pieces of your life (Jeremiah 18:1-6). He holds your life together with His unfailing love. In Part I, we discovered our God-given identity, worth, and name as His beloved daughters. In Part II let's explore typical areas of living by which we've developed broken images that resulted in or caused these broken pieces of our lives.

Lesson 11
Leaving

Walking Off....

The dreadful sin in our childhood was walking off, leaving the house without anyone knowing where you were. We'd play with the neighbors' children when we were not working the fields either for Big Daddy or on loan for some other farmer who didn't have this great working class called children. Curfew was dark. Whenever the sun started setting, we knew it was time to go home. We'd hear Mommy calling us from the front porch... Joe, Mary Lee, and so on until she'd called us all by name. Even if it was the second ending of a game, the game was over. We'd cut through the trail. My mind was flooded with the fears of wild animals and crawling snakes, which Mommy promised would seal our fate if we disobeyed. If we weren't killed on the trail, then Daddy was sure to take care of us when he returned from wherever he went past the boundaries of the neighborhood called Cottage Grove.

All I dreamed of was leaving. It didn't matter where I went.... I was going. I was waiting the day when I'd be brave enough to defy the rule of staying in the house, the yard, the field, even the neighborhood. I was going to walk off from the house and never come back. I wasn't going to ask permission and I would make sure no one knew where I was. My great escape came from college. I showed up with no career choice, no goals and no ambition burning in my soul other than leaving home and never returning. I knew I'd live without rules, without anyone keeping me in the yard, calling me home. I'd play with kids that lived a long way from our house and my neighborhood for as long as I desired no matter how dark it was. Today, I sit in the house where I grew up. I remember the care my parents took in raising us. Warm tears flood my face at the thought of the many children I have encountered who were raised without boundaries; who didn't know the trail which led to home and who had no fear of wild animals or crawling snakes. I did defy the rules… I walked off from my parent's teaching. I played with kids who lived far from the neighborhood of values where I grew up, and I did get lost not only from my family, but from myself and my God. I did encounter the wild animals, the snakes with poisonous bites which threatened my life. It was only through the blood of Jesus I survived. No matter how dark my life was I remained conscious, as my soul heard Mommy calling me by name and Daddy's sermons guiding me back through the trails to safety in the neighborhood, not Cottage Grove but the Kingdom of God. Hearing the voice of Mommy calling me by name and Daddy's sermons guided me back through the trails to safety and kept me conscious to the Kingdom of God.

When I taught school, it was common to find a student writing a word or a few words on his or her paper. Then in frustration try so hard to erase it until he or she tore a hole in the paper before crumpling it up to start again. No matter how hard I tried to convince him or her that it was ok, he or she would struggle with presenting imperfect work. God created man in His image and likeness. He looked in the earth and saw a nation of people who did not meet His standards for living. He did not relax his standards. He found one man, Noah, and compelled him to build an ark in preparation for His correction. He gave Noah the specifications by which to build, knowing that He would destroy mankind and every living thing not found therein. (Genesis 6:5-8 *NIV*)

When human beings began to increase in number on the earth and daughters were born to them, the sons of God saw that the daughters of humans were beautiful, and they married any of them they chose.

Then the LORD said, "My Spirit will not contend with humans forever, for they are mortal their days will be a hundred and twenty years." The Nephilim were on the earth in those days. Afterwards, the sons of God went to the daughters of humans and had children by them. They were the heroes of old, men of renown. The LORD saw how great the wickedness of humans had become on the earth, and that every inclination of the thoughts of the human heart was only evil all the time. The LORD regretted that He had made human beings on the earth, and His heart was deeply troubled. So the LORD said, "I will wipe from the face of the earth the human race I have created—and with them the animals, the birds and the creatures that move along the ground—for I regret that I have made them." But Noah found favor in the eyes of the LORD.

This is the account of Noah and his family. Noah was a righteous man, blameless among the people of his time, and he walked faithfully with God. Noah had three sons: Shem, Ham and Japheth. Now the earth was corrupt in God's sight and was full of violence. God saw how corrupt the earth had become, for all the people on earth had corrupted their ways.

So God said to Noah, "I am going to put an end to all people, for the earth is filled with violence because of them. I am surely going to destroy both them and the earth. So make yourself an ark, of cypress wood; make rooms in it and coat it with pitch inside and out." Having destroyed the works of His hands, and knowing that man would again distort His image, God makes a covenant with mankind to never destroy the earth again by flood. Seeing that mankind would never satisfy His desired standard for righteousness, He chose one Nation, the Jews to represent His Kingdom image in the earth. He tells them they are a holy nation, His royal priesthood, and called to show forth His image in the earth. When the Jews fail to satisfy His standard, He satisfies Himself with Himself and offers hope to all who will believe in salvation through His grace and mercy in the Godman Jesus.

"He was in the world, and the world was made by him, and the world knew him not. He came unto his own, and his own received him not. But as many as received him, to them gave the power to become the sons of God, even to them that believe on his name." (John 1:10-12 KJV)

A Call to Leave

In Genesis 12 God tells Abram to leave his father's house. He lived in a nation called Ur. Unlike me, he wasn't being urged to leave in search of fleshly pleasures and deceitful freedoms, which I found only to be prisons of the enemy's disguise. Abram was told to leave the influence of the other gods, whom his father worshipped. Abram was to follow the only true God. In his obedience, God would give him a new name, protect him and, through him, birth numerous nations.

In this same sense of leaving, God tells the man to leave his father and mother and cleave unto his wife as one flesh. What is this "one flesh" paradigm God is calling Abram to establish in leaving his father's house? It appears that Abram's father, Terah did set out to go to Canaan, the land promised to his people by God, after his son, Haran died in Ur (Genesis 11:28). He takes with him Abram, Sarai and Lot. Although he sets out to go, he somehow falls short of that place of promise. He settles in Haran (same name as his dead son), perhaps suggesting that he never got past the death of his son. Howbeit, God tells Abram to leave this place. Don't settle in this place... I have more for you (Gen. 11: 32). It takes much courage to leave the comfort of the familiar. Many like Terah have set out for more but find themselves settling in some place short of where God has destined for them and even dying there.

> It takes much courage to leave the comfort of the familiar in exchange for the unknown. Yet it's only in leaving that one becomes the express image of God.

When I was young it was common to watch folk sitting on the porch with dad talking about going somewhere. They would stand up say, "Better be going Rev (or my dad's nickname, Piggy, depending on the acquaintance)." They'd stand there for a few minutes as if to leave then sit down again. After several attempts to leave the person would eventually leave hours later. Leaving can sometimes be challenging, especially when we have no specific goals in mind. Abram is told to leave. He didn't have the carefully traced footprints of his father or mother, nor the trail through the woods leading to the safety of the family. His only compass echoed from his soul, a voice compelling him to journey to someplace away from his country, his kin, and his father's house. It would be in this unknown place that God would make his name great, bless him and allow him to be a blessing.

"Now the LORD had said unto Abram, Get thee out of thy country, and from thy kindred, and from thy father's house, unto a land that I will shew thee: 2 And I will make of thee a great nation, and I will bless thee, and make thy name great; and thou shalt be a blessing." (Genesis 12:1-2 KJV)

God wanted to expand Abram's existence beyond the shallow perceptions of lesser gods. In this sense of leaving he'd bring forth or give birth to nations having the same mindset as he. Though the call to another place was physical, more so it was spiritual; a place he could live out the abundance of God's will in the earth. For too long we have celebrated the good intentions of those who knew God desired more. How many like Abram's father or the folks who struggled to leave our front porch, for whatever reason, just never left? Only intentional people who are willing to leave the comforts of the porch, their acquaintances and the empty existence they've come to tolerate will obtain the promises of God.

Leaving and Letting Go: Our Sons and Daughters

We see the distinct results in *how* we choose to leave. "Walking off" is the premature attempt to seek the freedoms and gifts God's given us, while "A call to leave" positions us in God's favor and direction as we move toward what we are designed to do or become. One leads to detour and the other to destiny. Nevertheless, for those parents who are disappointed and discouraged with their own times of "leaving" or that of their children, I'd like to offer support.

Very recently I sat in the prayer house (an actual house I own that's dedicated as a community prayer facility) talking to a parent suffering the pain associated with a prodigal child. I thought of the pain I inflicted upon my dad especially as I encouraged her to back away. How clear in my memory the day dad determined that he was "putting me in the hands of the Lord." I didn't think too much of it at the time. As a matter of fact, I thought it would be good not having him hassle me about whatever or whoever. As I reached my hands out to pray with the parent, I knew without a doubt that it was time for her to let go and for God to step in. Last time I heard from her she was doing well and seeing the hand of God move in her life. Satan knew that eating of the forbidden fruit would allow the man and woman to see what happens on the earth through lustful desires, having their eyes opened perpetually to fleshly pleasures. Meaning, oftentimes, as parents, we are so focused on how the child isn't becoming what we desire or so focused on the mistakes of the child, we attach our affections on what we desire rather than focus on God's ability to restore and renew.

I remember crying while teaching at a session. I wept uncontrollably as I thought of the suffering my dad endured. Many in the room wept with me as I described my drive and

> The most important gift any parent can offer their children is clear and well-enforced boundaries.

passion for destroying the works of the enemy today. I, too, have been enslaved by satan's evil devices. Living in a world of relaxed morals and numerous socially accepted norms, it's essential that parents take the time and make intentional resolves to carefully establish the lines of the family divide. Although I defied the rules and became "scattered among other nations," it was the clear lines that distinguished my father's house from any other house which, in the end, caused me to desire my father's house as did the prodigal son (Luke 15).

The Prophet Jeremiah paints a portrait of the grief felt as God's chosen people are being carried away by their enemy. He uses Rachel, the more desired wife of Isaac to denote this image of non-consoled mourning. How many mothers have we attempted to console as they watch their children walk away or be carried away from the boundaries of their communities or neighborhoods? Although none could comfort Rachael, the Prophet offers hope in that her works would be rewarded.

"This is what the LORD says: "A voice is heard in Ramah, mourning and great weeping, Rachel weeping for her children and refusing to be comforted, because they are no more." 16 This is what the LORD says: "Restrain your voice from weeping and your eyes from tears, for your work will be rewarded," declares the LORD. "They will return from the land of the enemy. So there is hope for your descendants," declares the LORD. "Your children will return to their own land." (Jeremiah 31:15-17 NIV)

To parents like mine who have done all you know to do to raise your children, you should not be ashamed, feel guilty, or hopeless! And even if you didn't make all of the right choices in rearing them, the blame doesn't rest with you. There are enough Godly examples for them to know a better way. I bid you, let go! I know you've been to the altar many times and it seems as if God is not listening. He is listening and He promises to reward your work and bring them back. (Jeremiah 31:15-17 NIV)

I spend time talking to many young people. How clearly, I see in them that which dad saw in me years ago. The more you or I point out the flaws, the more satan closes their eyes to Godly wisdom in exchange for godly (small g) authority. Sometimes I sit quietly as each complain, "Folk (usually parents) don't get it". They plead their case as if standing before a judge and hoping that I'd at least get it and help open the eyes of those folk. As careful as a surgeon preparing to remove a deadly tumor, I shine the light on the speck, while remembering the beam which was in my own eyes. I watch as the doctor removes the speck, apply the balm and we both leave seeing. Jesus warns us that satan, calling him the thief comes to kill, steal, and destroy the lives of as many as he can deceive *(John 10:10 KJV)*. Though many of us have fallen victim to his devices, I'd like to testify that there's one at the river of life named Jesus who is giving sight to the blind. There is a balm in Gilead. *"Is there no balm in Gilead? Is there no physician there? Why then is there no healing for the wound of my people?" (Jeremiah 8:22 NIV)*

I tell my story in hopes that some parent will find comfort in knowing that their work has not been in vain. Remember, it's only so long that a true son or daughter will attempt to satisfy themselves with the pig's husk before he or she remembers their true identity and long to sit at the Father's table (Luke 15:13-17, NIV).

How I regret that my parents didn't get to embrace my new life. My mother died and was buried four days before I left for college and my dad died in the pulpit preaching the gospel, seven years later. However, I'll never forget the conversation with dad on the eve of his death. I called home, not sure why, but somewhere in the conversation he said, "I was just sitting here looking at your picture...You look so much like your dad," he continued. Then he said the words that confirmed his confidence in my return home. He said, "God has shown me your end, and I'm so proud of you." Then he concluded with, "Daddy loves you." I didn't know that this would be my dad's last words to me. My dad knew that one day I'd come to myself and return home. Heading home with still a distance to travel, my dad met me that night with a robe of love which covered my shame. He put a covenant ring of grace on my finger connecting me again to the family and gave me new shoes allowing me to walk again on the path of righteousness.

"I will set out and go back to my father and say to him: Father, I have sinned against heaven and against you. 19 I am no longer worthy to be called your son; make me like one of your hired servants.' So he got up and went to his father. "But while he was still a long way off, his father saw him and was filled with compassion for him; he ran to his son, threw his arms around him and kissed him. "The son said to him, 'Father, I have sinned against heaven and against you. I am no longer worthy to be called your son.' 22 "But the father said to his servants, 'Quick! Bring the best robe and put it on him. Put a ring on his finger and sandals on his feet." (Luke 15:18-22 (NIV)

The Prophet Jeremiah prophesied of a time that our sons would die so numerous that none would be able to gather them.

"Death has climbed in through our windows and has entered our fortresses; it has removed the children from the streets and the young men from the public squares. Say, "This is what the LORD declares: "Dead bodies will lie like dung on the open field, like cut grain behind the reaper, with no one to gather them." (Jeremiah 9:21-22 NIV)

Although our sons are dying in unprecedented numbers in our nation's streets, I believe at this same time God is commanding that the earth give up our sons and daughters. Many of you, as did my dad have awaited their return. Your prayers and tears have been heard. For a season they embraced the deceits of riches and the counterfeit freedoms offered in the world. Yet, many are awakening to their true identities and are rising to return to their healthy homes and neighborhoods. No matter how far away they were removed from your house and the neighborhood, God will gather them.

"See, I will bring them from the land of the north and gather them from the ends of the earth. Among them will be the blind and the lame, expectant mothers and women in labor; a great throng will return. They will come with weeping; they will pray as I bring them back. I will lead them beside streams of water on a level path where they will not stumble, because I am Israel's father, and Ephraim is my firstborn son.

"Hear the word of the LORD, you nations; proclaim it in distant coastlands: 'He who scattered Israel will gather them and will watch over his flock like a shepherd.' For the LORD will deliver Jacob and redeem them from the hand of those stronger than they." (Jeremiah 31:8-11 NIV)

I believe the house of God will be filled with true worshippers and our streets will be inhabited and no longer desolate. Those of us who will extend ourselves to others and stand strong to build Zion's walls will be called the repairers of the breach and will restore safety to our Nation. (Isaiah 58:10-12).

Lesson 12
Cleaving as One Flesh

God tells man to leave his father and mother and cleave to his wife becoming again one flesh (*Genesis 2:24*). This passage gives us God's perception of marriage. In Part One we explored how in the beginning God made man and woman as one flesh, man. One flesh man was able to subdue and have dominion over the earth. However, man could not fulfill God's full command as one flesh in that he could not be fruitful and multiply, filling the earth with people having the image and likeness of God (Genesis 1:28).

In Part I, we discovered that man recognized a need for something outside of himself as he names the animals and watches them bring forth after their own kind. Being fully aware of his inability to please God in his current state, man doesn't go to sleep (suggesting rest) God puts him to sleep. In this place of discontent, many men and women of God fail. When flesh man tries to satisfy spirit God knowing not the plan of God, he, as other creatures, bring forth of his own kind rather than the image of spiritual God. While man slept God takes one of his ribs and makes woman. He brings the woman to the man and he names her woman saying she was taken from me. Man must see woman as a part of him. Although she is separate and complete in and of herself, man must accept her spirit, that part of her which is created in the image of God as his own. However, after the fall, we will find man no longer seeing the woman as a part of him, and thus assigning his wife the name Eve because she would be the mother of all living. While Eve has the ability to bear children, without this spiritual oneness with Adam, the image of God would be missing. I'll explore this concept more in Part III.

When God sees mankind in the earth, He looks for one flesh. Therefore, He has much to say about relationships, offenses, and even hindrance to prayers when there is discord (I Peter 3:7). Although your children may resemble you in the flesh, God sees them as separate nations. They are free to operate under totally different authorities than you. You have no voice in a child's life once they leave home or they are married. Far too many marriages are adversely affected because parental influences are not left behind. While we pray that our influences have been healthy, it's ultimately the child's choices which determine the outcomes of their lives. Even though Abram had been raised in an environment in which God was not honored, he was given the opportunity to leave and become the father of God-honoring nations. Every person is seen as a nation with the freedom to choose their own rules or authorities. Each must decide what authority he or she will be subject to. Although we live in a society which seems chaotic and spiraling toward destruction, God still gives mankind the freedom to choose. Though we have the freedom to choose, how essential it is to be reminded that all will have to give an account of his or her choices.

The idea of cleaving has to do with the joining of the man and woman as one through the act of sexual intimacy (a concept which was not introduced until after marriage). God sees marriage as a covenant and the sexual act as the consummation of the covenant with the shedding of blood. Therefore, chastity was honorable and even punishable by death in the Old Testament.

"If a man takes a wife and, after sleeping with her, dislikes her and slanders her and gives her a bad name, saying, "I married this woman, but when I approached her, I did not find proof of her virginity," then the young woman's father and mother shall bring to the town elders at the gate proof that she was a virgin.

Her father will say to the elders, "I gave my daughter in marriage to this man, but he dislikes her. Now he has slandered her and said, 'I did not find your daughter to be a virgin.' But here is the proof of my daughter's virginity." Then her parents shall display the cloth before the elders of the town, and the elders shall take the man and punish him. They shall fine him a hundred shekels of silver and give them to the young woman's father, because this man has given an Israelite virgin a bad name. She shall continue to be his wife; he must not divorce her as long as he lives.

If, however, the charge is true and no proof of the young woman's virginity can be found, she shall be brought to the door of her father's house and there the men of her town shall stone her to death. She has done an outrageous thing in Israel by being promiscuous while still in her father's house. You must purge the evil from among you."
(Deut.22:13-21 NIV)

Although the punishment of that day was excessive, we must not conclude that God has relaxed His standards regarding premarital sex. While there's not the physical death imposed there is, in fact, spiritual death or separation from God imposed immediately. There's a strong impulse for young girls to give away their virginity before the marriage. This is the enemy's way of weakening or confusing the sanctity of family and undermining the authority of the home and pleasure of worship. The Apostle Paul warns Christians to avoid committing sin against our own bodies as he urges us to flee fornication.

*"Do you not know that your bodies are members of Christ himself? Shall I then take the members of Christ and unite them with a prostitute? Never! Do you not know that he who unites himself with a prostitute is one with her in body? For it is said, "The two will become one flesh." But whoever is united with the Lord is one with him in spirit. Flee from sexual immorality. All other sins a person commits are outside the body, but whoever sins sexually, sins against their own body."
(1 Corinthians 6:15-18 NIV)*

Lesson 13
Submission

Perhaps Jesus' expressed need to go through Samaria to Galilee was not directional, but also purposeful. Was He driven by the need for the gospel to spread beyond the cultural divides of the Jews and Samaritans? I'd like to confer that the Master purposely positions Himself at Jacob's well knowing that the woman he'd encounter there would come. Tired and weary from His travel, Christ sits on the well seemingly at the mercy of those who would come. Purposefully sending away those who would assist or oppose Him, He crosses the cultural lines and compels the woman to give Him a drink though she questions His authority to cross-cultural divides to ask her for water.

"So he left Judea and went back once more to Galilee. Now he had to go through Samaria. So he came to a town in Samaria called Sychar, near the plot of ground Jacob had given to his son Joseph. Jacob's well was there, and Jesus, tired as he was from the journey, sat down by the well. It was about noon.

When a Samaritan woman came to draw water, Jesus said to her, "Will you give me a drink?" 8 (His disciples had gone into the town to buy food.) 9 The Samaritan woman said to him, "You are a Jew and I am a Samaritan woman. How can you ask me for a drink?" (For Jews do not associate with Samaritans. (John 4:3-9 NIV)

Jesus offers her the opportunity to know Him beyond laws which prohibited her from having such knowledge of Him or conversation with Him. Jesus exposes her lack of knowledge saying, "Had you known me, you would have asked me for living water so that you won't have to continue to come here at the 6th hour for water." Not knowing who He was, she asked Him how He would be able to give her water when He didn't have anything to draw with Himself. She then explores His claim of authority beyond that of

Jacob who gave them the well and even he and his family and cattle drank from the same. All the woman knew was the limitations of seeking to satisfy her physical thirst from this well. However, the Master spoke of satisfying a spiritual thirst which precludes one from the need to seek to satisfy oneself with things which can never satisfy fully. The woman being thirsty for more, asked the Master for the living water.

"Jesus answered her, "If you knew the gift of God and who it is that asks you for a drink, you would have asked him, and he would have given you living water." "Sir," the woman said, "you have nothing to draw with and the well is deep. Where can you get this living water? Are you greater than our father Jacob, who gave us the well and drank from it himself, as did also his sons and his livestock?" Jesus answered, "Everyone who drinks this water will be thirsty again, but whoever drinks the water I give them will never thirst. Indeed, the water I give them will become in them a spring of water welling up to eternal life." The woman said to him, "Sir, give me this water so that I won't get thirsty and have to keep coming here to draw water." (John 4:10-15 NIV)

Though many speak of Him, few dare to move beyond the earthly laws which separate, and divide- satisfying a need to know Him and cleave to Him in spiritual unity. It's only as one hunger and thirsts for the Master that he or she will be filled with the full knowledge of who He is (Matthew 5:6, NIV).

Sensing a desire for this water, the woman asks the Master to give her a drink. Could He possibly have something which would satisfy her thirst and keep her from this place of lack? Although He offers her the drink, He tells her first to go get her husband, and come back (John 4:16, NIV). Every time a man and a woman come together intimately, he and she consummate a union with the potential for forming a nation. This nation has the potential of bringing forth other nations. Jesus knew that the woman could never satisfy her desire for true worship with Him in her current state. In order to satisfy her desire for worship, He prompts her to inner truth. He asks her to go get her husband the one with whom she'd established authority and spiritual unity. The woman answered saying, "I have no husband." Christ answers, "You've had five husbands, and the one you are with now is still not your husband" (John 4:17-18, NIV).

In other words, the Master tells this poor woman that she could not be in a marriage covenant with Him, nor could she attain true worship as long as she misunderstood or was not submitted in a relational covenant. She apparently knew something about worship, as she told him she knew where the Jews and Samaritans worshipped. She could even tell Him who they worshipped. It's easy to go to church, lift our hands in worship and still not be in true covenant with God. The Master calls this woman to acknowledge and renounce all previous authorities and covenants made in the flesh. Such freedom allows her to surrender to His ultimate authority resulting in true worship and obedience. He tells her that He knows about the Jew's and the Samaritans' worship and even where they worshipped. Yet all was in vain because it was not in the spirit of truth (John 4:17-24).

88

The scripture tells us that when the spirit of truth comes, He will reveal all things to us (John 16:13). Before we can build Christian homes and churches, we must submit to one authority. We can't continue to submit willingly or even unwillingly to lesser gods. It's impossible for a wife to submit in marriage unless she has first learned true submission to God. She must be married to Him in every sense of His unyielding authority. Submission must never be limited to the woman or the wife. God never intended submission to be solely the woman's response in marriage. Paul clearly tells us that submission is mutual as he urges to man and woman to submit to one another.

"Submit to one another out of reverence for Christ. Wives submit yourselves to your own husbands as you do to the Lord."
(Ephesians 5:21-22 NIV)

Although Jesus tells His disciples that He must go through Samaria, He never physically goes beyond the well. He knew if this one woman drank from His well that her message would spark a hunger for the transforming message throughout Samaria, starting with Kingdom man. Jesus tells the

> It's easy to go church even lift our hands seemingly in worship and still not be in true covenant with God. True Worship comes only as one acknowledges the truth in the inward parts.

woman that the hour has come for true worship. The woman knew that the Messiah who was to come would bring such truth and present worship which crosses the racial, cultural, and even doctrinal divides we find in our churches which lend way to biases and hatred. Just as God gives woman the nature to give birth physically, she is called upon at this hour to bring forth spiritually as well. The Godly woman's willingness to submit to God's authority has saved many marriages and homes. Once the woman of Samaria was able to understand true worship those living outside the authority of the gospel were drawn as she compelled men saying, "Come meet a man who told me all I ever did," she continues in humble submission, "Is not this the Christ?" My sisters we can't continue to try and manipulate our men or husbands to come to Christ. Let's restrain from the tracks in his pockets, in the coffee cups and on his pillow. The message can't be dropped here or there in subtle conversations. The men of Samaria came to meet Christ because the woman was bold enough to share her personal message supported by the Word of God (John 4:28-30). The woman leaves her pot and goes back into the city compelling men to come. The time has come, and our message is intense. Christ is in search of thirsty men and women and He's purposely positioning Himself for such encounters.

Lesson 14
Singlehood

Mankind was created to show forth God's image in the earth. Whether married or single, we are called to bring to light the invisible Kingdom of God before a dark and perverse generation. The majority of society has considered the idea of marriage at some time…Who should I marry? Is marriage for me? Will I be successful in marriage? Am I getting too old? In the next section, I will explore in depth the concept of Marriage. However, some attention must be given to living single before we can fully understand God's view of marriage.

Although God created both male and female, for a period of time man was fulfilling the mandates of God alone. God refers to man's aloneness as not good, yet He allows it to be so for a time. God knew that in His timing He would unveil His desired plan for man and woman. Knowing that God never does anything without a purpose and seeing that He didn't just make man and woman as a separate being from the start, I must conclude that there was an

> One of the primary reasons for so few successful marriages is that one or both partners have not been successful at being single or alone with God.

essential need for man's temporary state of aloneness. It was during this time that man is allowed to operate in his God-given authority, assigning names to every creature in the earth. To further conclude that man was exclusively alone in the process, He said that whatever name man assigned to any creature that was ultimately their name.

91

"The LORD God said, "It is not good for the man to be alone. I will make a helper suitable for him." Now the LORD God had formed out of the ground all the wild animals and all the birds in the sky. He brought them to the man to see what he would name them; and whatever the man called each living creature, that was its name. So the man gave names to all the livestock, the birds in the sky and all the wild animals. But for Adam no suitable helper was found." (Genesis 2:18-20 NIV)

Although the woman was not visible at this time in creation, she was still an integral part of the naming process. Because the woman was inside of man, the feminine nature was present as man differentiated between the various creatures. Perhaps, it's because of the tendency to allow variables outside of us, especially other people to influence our decisions is why God allowed man to complete such a vital task alone. Having never married, the Apostle Paul recommended a single life in lieu of marriage arguing that the single man or woman is free to focus on fully pleasing God rather than having the distractions of pleasing others especially their spouses.

"Are you pledged to a woman? Do not seek to be released. Are you free from such a commitment? Do not look for a wife. But if you do marry, you have not sinned; and if a virgin marries, she has not sinned. But those who marry will face many troubles in this life, and I want to spare you this....

I would like you to be free from concern. An unmarried man is concerned about the Lord's affairs—how he can please the Lord. But a married man is concerned about the affairs of this world—how he can please his wife—and his interests are divided. An unmarried woman or virgin is concerned about the Lord's affairs: Her aim is to be devoted to the Lord in both body and spirit. But a married woman is concerned about the affairs of this world—how she can please her husband. I am saying this for your own good, not to restrict you, but that you may live in a right way in undivided devotion to the Lord." **(***1 Corinthians 7:25-28; 32-35 NIV)*

Many individuals choose marriage over singlehood because of their struggle with sexual desires. When the new believers at Corinth asked Paul about sex, marriage, and immorality, he offers marriage as a probable solution because of the Corinthians' strong tendency toward immoral living. However, such recommendations have never been God's perfect will for man, nor was Paul suggesting it to be.

"Now for the matters you wrote about: "It is good for a man not to have sexual relations with a woman." But since sexual immorality is occurring, each man should have sexual relations with his own wife, and each woman with her own husband. The husband should fulfill his marital duty to his wife, and likewise the wife to her husband. The wife does not have authority over her own body but yields it to her husband. In the same way, the husband does not have authority over his own body but yields it to his wife. Do not deprive each other except perhaps by mutual consent and for a time, so that you may devote yourselves to prayer. Then come together again so that Satan will not tempt you because of your lack of self-control. I say this as a concession, not as a command." (1 Corinthians 7:1-6 NIV)

Married individuals should never be perceived as having preferred dominance over those choosing to be single. All of mankind is created in the image of God and called to glorify God whatever their state.

Lesson 15
Marriage

Marriages struggle when couples are not able to grasp or have failed to embrace this concept of oneness before marriage. Successful marriages exist when Kingdom minded couples are free to make decisions that are spirit derived rather than those of fleshly male or female presumptions. Many marriages are viewed as creation components in that one or both partners see the other as making him or her complete in some form. Marriage must be the merging of two complete individuals as one to manifest the desire of God for Kingdom reproduction whether naturally or spiritually. There must be the continual yielding of both partners for the higher expression of good not based on natural or physical evaluations, but rather on spiritual mandates which were determined while alone with God before marriage.

As mentioned in the previous section, Paul (1 Corinthians 7:2-5) suggested marriage as a possible solution to fleshly lust. While marriage is not in and of itself the remedy for sexual expressions, I do say that consenting sexual pleasures are not only permissible but are highly recommended for the success of marriage. Though not married, Paul never concludes that marriage was not a good option for some. When we see the rising number of marriages (even Christian marriages) which end in divorce we tend to echo the sentiments of the Apostle. Divorce has never been the remedy for poor marriages, and Jesus clarified that Moses only allows divorce because mankind's heart was hard and unforgiving. Paul encourages the believing spouse to not divorce the unbelieving spouse, arguing that the sanctity of the marriage is preserved by the believing spouse in that the Lord views them as one.

"To the rest I say this (I, not the Lord): If any brother has a wife who is not a believer and she is willing to live with him, he must not divorce her. And if a woman has a husband who is not a believer and he is willing to live with her; she must not divorce him. For the unbelieving husband has been sanctified through his wife, and the unbelieving wife has been sanctified through her believing husband. Otherwise your children would be unclean, but as it is, they are holy. But if the unbeliever leaves, let it be so. The brother or the sister is not bound in such circumstances; God has called us to live in peace. How do you know, wife, whether you will save your husband? Or, how do you know, husband, whether you will save your wife?" **(***1 Corinthians 7:12-16 NIV***)**

Thus, I applaud the few men and women of God who have committed themselves to each other and to God's plan for their marriage, despite the struggle, testing, and pruning that marriage affords. Those unions that survive have God as the third member of their relationship and, thus, are witnesses and expressions of divine expressions of godly marriages. In turn, those unions give birth to families that are Kingdom-built and Kingdom-minded. Now, I'm not offering commentary on the various types of struggles a marriage may face or making judgment on the marriages that did not survive, despite a partner's commitment to the institution of marriage or the invitation of God in the marriage. I can say, however, that any form of abuse is not the will of God in any relationship, and I must support that individual seeking safety. Abusive relationships, physical or emotional, impedes one's freedom to worship God, as He has not called us to such bondage. Professional counseling is needed for both individuals and as a couple or family, once safety and a degree of trust are re-established.

Paul had much to say to the Corinthians not only about being single or married, but also about worship in general. When asked about proper order in worship, Paul talked about the need for women to cover their heads in reverence to Christ and man's God-given authority.

"But I want you to realize that the head of every man is Christ, and the head of the woman is man, and the head of Christ is God. Every man who prays or prophesies with his head covered dishonors his head. 5 But every woman who prays or prophesies with her head uncovered dishonors her head—it is the same as having her head shaved. For if a woman does not cover her head, she might as well have her hair cut off; but if it is a disgrace for a woman to have her hair cut off or her head shaved, then she should cover her head. A man ought not to cover his head, since he is the image and glory of God; but woman is the glory of man. For man did not come from woman, but woman from man; neither was man created for woman, but woman for man. It is for this reason that a woman ought to have authority over her own head, because of the angels." (1 Corinthians 11:3-10 NIV)

Although the Apostle refers to the order of creation as his source, he relents freedom to these believers as he suggests that they judge for themselves the necessity for women to be covered or uncovered in worship. He doesn't suggest man's superiority over woman or hers over the man in that he concludes that both man and woman came from each other and everything comes from God.

"Nevertheless, in the Lord woman is not independent of man, nor is man independent of woman. For as woman came from man, so also man is born of woman. But everything comes from God. Judge for yourselves: Is it proper for a woman to pray to God with her head uncovered?"

96

(1 Corinthians 11:11-13 NIV)

I make mention of this worship concept at this time to share the importance of personal choice in marriage. There's not a blueprint for marriage, and one may differ intrinsically from another, yet both be pleasing to God. The concept of submission is rarely viewed from the perception as unto the Lord. Therefore, a faulty worldview of submission has plagued mankind and even Christian audiences for some time. The Apostle Paul addressed the concept of submission in Ephesus as he encouraged husbands and wives to submit to one another in reverence to God (Ephesians 5:21). As questions of submission continue to be answered or viewed from fleshly postures then mankind single or married will fail to bring forth the Godly witness needed in the earth. How easy it is to submit one to another regardless of gender or authority when we have learned submission to God while alone with Him. The ultimate question of every believer must be, "Lord, what would you have me to do?" ... Then, in response to a Holy God be as Mary, the mother of the awaited Messiah who when favored to give birth to Christ, submitted humbly saying, "Be it to me as you have said" (Luke 1:38, NIV).

Lesson 16
Sin's Deception

Sin has a way of promising much but taking more. Satan never attempted to tempt man with fruit from the forbidden tree. What did he see in the nature of woman which signaled the possibility for such allure? Could he have noticed her sheepish demeanor as she spoke to man? Was perhaps it found in her discontent in tasks? Was she constantly moving things around, looking for something bigger or better? What was the clue? How did he know then and how does he know now?

The Bible admonishes us to be alert. Keep always in mind that the devil is not your friend. He is your adversary (enemy) and he walks to and fro in the earth seeking whom he can devour (1 *Peter 5:8, NIV*). Although I will share God's plan for redemption in Part Three, it's imperative that we are not deceived again by his tactics. To avoid such demise, we must have knowledge. In Part One I shared the concept of being made. There is godly confidence which is emitted from those who have their identity confirmed in the finished works of Christ. The woman became distracted by the earth and its fullness. Although she had been given the authority to share in ordering and keeping it, she allowed the earth to rule over her. She thought something outside of God working in and through her could make her more complete or better. The woman not confident in who she was in God gave the devil the opportunity to tempt her.

Let's take a look at this spiral decline…The enemy's first assault was through attacking the integrity of God and His

Word as he explores the woman's view of the absolute authority of God's Word.

"Now the serpent was more crafty than any of the wild animals the LORD God had made. He said to the woman, "Did God really say, 'You must not eat from any tree in the garden'?" The woman said to the serpent, "We may eat fruit from the trees in the garden, but God did say, 'You must not eat fruit from the tree that is in the middle of the garden, and you must not touch it, or you will die.' " "You will not certainly die," the serpent said to the woman." (Genesis 3:1-4 NIV)

The woman responds with the truth of the Word but is careless as she allows the enemy to manipulate the absolute authority of God's Word, saying, "You shall not surely die." He suggests some form of death but not ultimate. If he can get us to misinterpret the Word by adding or taking away from its intent, he knows that he has an entryway to our heart. We are instructed to guard ourselves against the opposing issues which arise as we leave our hearts unprotected. Proverbs 4:23 says "Above all else, guard your heart, for everything you do flows from it" (*NIV*).

As a shield against sin, the Psalmist writes, *"Thy word have I hid in mine heart, that I might not sin against thee." (Psalm 119:11, KJV).* When the enemy sees that he can have the woman question the authority and truthfulness of God's Word, he knows he had an entryway into her heart. He continues his advance by causing her to question her completeness in God by suggesting that the forbidden fruit would give her more insight into the things of God... even good and evil (Genesis 3:5). The ultimate victory came as the woman came to see the earth through the enemy's world view. Even knowing

99

that she has to her avail all the trees of the garden for food, she sees the once forbidden tree as pleasant, desirable, and having the potential to *MAKE* her wise.

"When the woman saw that the fruit of the tree was good for food and pleasing to the eye, and also desirable for gaining wisdom, she took some and ate it. She also gave some to her husband, who was with her, and he ate it." (Genesis 3:6 NIV)

The enemy always appeal to our fleshly nature. When we fail to allow the Bible to be our ultimate and foundational truth, and who we are is derived from any source outside of God, then we give place to his deceptions. Not only did she eat, but she gave also to her husband who also eats, and their eyes were open to see nakedness which God never intended.

Lesson 17
Nakedness and Shame

Love is Blind.

A common expression often used in relationships. I remember the many times my folks were sure I was under some spell. Though Daddy taught against the phenomenon of voodoo, he was starting to think there was some truth to it as far as I was concerned. He needed something to explain my blindness as well as that of some of my siblings. When satan approaches the woman to eat of the forbidden fruit, he promises that their eyes would be opened, and they would be as gods, knowing good and evil. As mentioned in the previous lesson, the idea of having a godly perspective, appealed to the woman and she now sees that which was once forbidden as now being capable of satisfying her physical desires, aesthetic nature, and ability to provide earthly wisdom. There was not a need for clothing for the man and woman were innocent, pure, and in perfect communion with God before the fall. The bible says that the man and woman were naked and not ashamed.

"Adam and his wife were both naked, and they felt no shame."
(Genesis 2:25 NIV)

Whatever appearances of nakedness there were from the beginning, the couple suspected no need to cover up the cracks, the chipped edges, or the wear that imposes itself upon any vessel just through life processes. The man and woman were created to live forever- free from the need to apologize, repent, or feel inferior. Each could live in full assurance that they were the expressed image of God in the earth. The enemy's deceptions had now driven the once full and complete man and woman in search of coverings as he and she crotched in shame and ruin. Perhaps, we can sense they're lost, especially that of the woman as we shall explore further in the story of Naomi in Part III.

The man and woman were experiencing shame for the first time. Something was dreadfully wrong and neither knew what to do to correct it. The enemy had promised the woman that her eyes would be opened and that she would be as God, knowing good and evil even suggesting a misunderstanding of the Word of God. He agreed that they would die... but not for real dead, only their eyes would open. The enemy knew that man would have an openness to concepts which clearly opposed God's commandments.

> They each saw in each other and themselves the naked truth of mankind's earthly existence apart from God.

"You will not certainly die," the serpent said to the woman. "For God knows that when you eat from it your eyes will be opened, and you will be like God, knowing good and evil." (Genesis 3:4-5 NIV)

We no longer view sin as rebellion against a Holy God, but rather an alternate lifestyle, freedom permitted by those who desire to live life uninhibited if it doesn't harm another. Man who lives apart from God still moves in the earth in some basic form of existence. Therefore those who are void of the true imagery and purposes of God assume that He is of some noteworthy progeny. This negligent life view allows for a casual, perhaps occasional involvement with God while reverencing as heroes or superstars those who present more or better apart from God as desirable. Why does this compelling desire for more bring now shame and confusion of mind to the couple? While discussing the topic of the "Fall in the Garden" to the children at our church, one of the students asked, "Why did God create the devil anyway?" Her frustration was noted in the contortion that eclipsed the beauty of her face, as she awaited my answer. Acknowledging her agony, I simply replied, "Honey, He wants your love for Him to be so certain that He gave you a choice." Although we don't always make the best decisions, God allows us the freedom to choose. When one is allowed to choose, they're given a sense of power which is not afforded with compulsion. Those who choose to follow after righteousness do so out of a true hunger for God and His commandments, in the face of various temptations. The forbidden fruit when consumed gave way to an insatiable hunger which could never be satisfied, as does all temptations which once conceived... brings forth sin and death.

"Blessed is the one who perseveres under trial because, having stood the test, that person will receive the crown of life that the Lord has promised to those who love him. When tempted, no one should say, "God is tempting me." For God cannot be tempted by evil, nor does he tempt anyone; but each person is tempted when they are dragged away by their own evil desire and enticed. Then, after desire has conceived, it gives birth to sin; and sin, when it is full-grown, gives birth to death." (James 1:12-15 NIV)

Lesson 18
Choice

Knowing their current quandary, the man and woman attempt to cover their nakedness. Finding fig leaves as an available resource in the garden, they gather the leaves and carefully sew them together. The couple carefully drape the handmade garments about their frames, still feeling the chill of exposure which drives them deeper into the garden, hiding among the trees. The man and woman did all they could to cover their nakedness and shame, but to no avail. As fig leaves the lone solution to their plight, the couple assumes a perpetual existence hiding from God and each other.

Let's explore more attentively the fig leaves which served as the best alternative to that which was lacking or preferred. Often Christians suggest permissive versus a perfect

> We can only present the true image of God when He's the only thing that can be seen.

will of God theory in an attempt to cover as fig leaves the naked truth of falling short of God's glory. How much Christian service and church attendance is perhaps our way of covering up? With their eyes open to the nakedness, God never intended to be seen or known. Man and woman sought to hide not only from one another, but more importantly from God. The voice of God which previously brought them comfort and unity drove them to hide. When we move away from the foundational truth of God's Word, we seek to compensate for life with something lesser. They hid among the trees. Mankind attempts to cover his or her nakedness among the trees. Are the overcrowded schedules, immense church work, and unintentional deceptions shadowing you from the trees which we use to cover that which we're hiding from God? How can we be so busy and still not have His presence? Have we settled for the absence of His presence as shared in Part One? As long as our true identity is cloaked in some tangible worth or value system, then mankind will never know us as the people of God we were created to be. When God calls His people to come from among them, promising to be their God, and they His people, He's imposing upon those who'd dare leave, the opportunity to give birth to His image.

"Wherefore come out from among them, and be ye separate, saith the Lord, and touch not the unclean thing; and I will receive you."
(2 Corinthians 6:17 KJV)

Rarely does one see a true picture of God. Far too often His image is overcast by exhaustive church service which professes greatness but yields only cheap counterfeits. I wanted to know God, but I feared the cost. Could I bear the naked shame of letting go of all the things that made me appear great in the eyes of others? I'd worked so hard to obtain whatever I thought I had. Could I bear the scrutiny of those who'd certainly question my relationship with the Father? I'd been so much a part of the teaching that led the church world to think of certain things as God and others as not. How could I take off the priestly robe in return for a humble existence? With the "what if's" racing through my mind, I felt the robe slip from my shoulders and crumple to the floor around my feet. Fighting against the urge to pull it up again and shuttering from the coldness of being naked, I turn to the Father trembling in fear, knowing of a certainty that I'm in the right place.

Not being accustomed to this level of submission, I wept. I didn't know if the tears were from the fear of the unknown or from being naked. Although I wanted to hide, I resisted the fig leaves and set my eyes toward the places I'd been. I didn't know what I'd say…I only knew I'd answered a priestly call.

"I have surely heard Ephraim's moaning: 'You disciplined me like an unruly calf, and I have been disciplined. Restore me, and I will return, because you are the LORD my God. After I strayed, I repented; after I came to understand, I beat my breast. I was ashamed and humiliated because I bore the disgrace of my youth.' Is not Ephraim my dear son, the child in whom I delight? Though I often speak against him, I still remember him. Therefore, my heart yearns for him; I have great compassion for him," declares the LORD. "Set up road signs; put up guideposts. Take note of the highway, the road that you take. Return, Virgin Israel, return to your towns. How long will you wander, unfaithful Daughter Israel? The LORD will create a new thing on earth— the woman will return to the man."
(Jeremiah 31:18-22 NIV 37)

PART II

LESSON REVIEW

LIFE CHANGING TRUTHS

- Boundaries are Essential- The most important gift any parent can offer their children is clear and well-enforced boundaries.

- Leaving- It takes much courage to leave the comfort of the familiar in exchange for the unknown. Yet, it's only in leaving that one becomes the express image of God.

- Cleaving- Though many speak of the Master, few embrace the need to know and cleave to Him in Spiritual Unity.

- True Worship- It's easy to go to church and even lift our hands seemingly in worship and still not be in true covenant with God. True Worship comes only as one acknowledges truth in the inward parts.

- On Being Single or Married- The primary reason that there are so few successful marriages is that one or both partners have not been successful at being single or alone with God.

- Submission- As questions of submission continue to be answered or viewed from fleshly postures then mankind, single or married will fail to bring forth the Godly witness needed in the earth. How easy it is to submit one to another regardless of gender or authority when we have learned submission to God while alone with Him.

- Shame- The man and woman were experiencing shame for the first time. They each saw in each other and themselves the naked truth of earthly mankind's existence apart from God. Something was dreadfully wrong and neither knew what to do to correct it.

- Choice- Although we don't always make the best decisions, God allows us the freedom to choose. When allowed to choose, you're given a sense of power which is not afforded with compulsion. Those who choose to follow righteousness do so out of a true hunger for God and His commandments in the face of various temptations.

- Fig Leaves/Hiding- Are the overcrowded schedules, immense church work, and unintentional deceptions shadows from the trees which we use to cover that we're hiding from God? How can we be so busy and still not have His Presence?

PART III

ALL THINGS NEW

INTRODUCTION

I'll Arise and Go to My Father's House...

Although my dad had given me a ring and the robe on the
eve of his death, not all the neighborhood welcomed my
return. He was no longer around to validate my integrity.
My family was gradually seeing the change in me and was
coming to trust that it was more than an impressive act. To
gather as many supporters of my faith, I poured myself into
the study of God's Word. My initial goal was not to know
more about God's saving grace, neither was it to understand
and invest more in my personal decision for Him. I wanted
to articulate to a broader audience especially those who
doubted my conversion that both God and I were real.
Although my motives were not upfront at the start, I found
that the more I sought Him, the more I wanted Him and to
be like Him. Surprisingly, those who saw it hardest to
welcome me were members of the church world. Often, I
found myself working harder and harder to convince this
audience that I was worthy of their fellowship. I wondered if
the resistance I often encountered was because of where I'd
been, or that I was a woman in a male-dominated religious
culture. Nevertheless, there was some law or system of
thought in this community leaving me exhausted in works
and lacking in spiritual fulfillment. Seemingly, the more God
invited me to sit at His feet and learn of Him, the inward
burden of proof became lesser. I found myself utterly
exhausted and hungry as I sought to satisfy my soul's hunger
with less than the Father's meat. I knew what life was like at

the Father's house; I'd eaten from His table and recognized the provisions I missed while in this far country.

In Luke Chapter 15, the Bible tells us the story of the lost son who is more commonly known as the prodigal son. We note that the father gives his son all the blessings and goods which are due to him. He then allows his son the freedom to waste them in any way he chose. This freedom is most difficult for parents, especially for those who have not yielded everything to the Master and trusted in His ultimate plan. It was the father's willingness to allow his son the freedom to choose his path, regardless of how reckless his son would soon prove to be. The son realized that he was impoverished through his own choices not due to any lack in his father. The son then made a similar and intentional decision to arise and go back to his *father's house*. The son's decision is not derived through coercion, threats, or persuasions, but more importantly from a desire for his father and all that he knew him to be. The son's decision to return garnered different and opposing responses from the father and the older brother. While the father welcomed his son with a robe, ring, and shoes, the older brother responded with anger and resentment. Although there continued to be varied reactions to my return, I abandoned the need to be validated because many will never know the integrity of my heart. However, as the Psalmist noted in Psalm 139:23-24, daily I ask the Master to search me and know my thoughts and continually choose for me the paths which please Him.

Jesus addresses this issue of people's acceptance and rejection in John 14:1-3. John writes of Jesus' response to

His disciples seeing the immense sorrow they felt at the notice of His departure. The Master lends them hope as He encourages them to believe not only in God but also in Him… being forever reminded of His love for them. If our accusers know not the Father nor the Son who was sent to bear the image of the invisible God, how can they possibly know those who are born of Him? He not only tells His disciples to believe, He tells them that He would go ahead of them to prepare a place for them in His House where they could forever be in His presence (*John 14:1-3*). It's not our responsibility to get people to believe in us. We are to be the living proof that there is a God though man can't see Him. Although many still doubt my place in the earth, I believe that the Master has a place for me and all of those who are awaiting His return. I'm so thankful that my dad made provisions for his children. Through his abounding love for God, we have come to find rest in the faith he taught us to embrace. As I labor to finish the work the Father has sent me to do, I pray that my children will follow the path which leads to the Father's House. I pray that we all will make our return back to the Father as He is preparing His return for us.

Lesson 19
Returning

Following in the vein of God's sustenance, approval and acceptance from my narrative, let's look deeper and consider another narrative of returning home. In the first chapter in the book of Ruth, Naomi lost it all! Everything that made her feel whole and full of life had been buried someplace she'd never even intended to go. For a time, she was living the life... married, two sons and living in Bethel; which in the Greek language meant the *House of Bread*. What happens when the place you thought would forever be your place of provision ceases to provide, and you face a famine? Like most people who find themselves in such a crisis, Naomi's husband Elimelech seeks other arrangements for his family. I'm not sure how he comes about knowledge. Perhaps it was while sitting in the town square among his brethren that this husband and father hears that there's food in Moab. Surely the conversations in the square had been about how bad things were. Everybody was facing crop failures, and no one could give to another because all suffered need. It was out of this place of desperation that Elimelech against all previous reservations about Moab decides to move his family there. Evidently, he thought it to be a temporary move. Perhaps he'd told his friends the same thing, or even told Naomi when she protested leaving her friends behind, "We will come back when things are better, honey." The scriptures do not tell us what happened or even when it happened, but we do know that Elimelech dies in Moab without getting back to the place to which he'd promise to return. Before you judge him too quickly, I'd like to say a few words on behalf of the dead. I also left. As I shared in the previous chapter, I walked off and went to "Moab" ... a God forbidden place. Moab promises much to all who enters and there, the grass always appears greener.

The few like me who survived its prison and are left to tell the story know only too well the fate of Elimelech and his sons. Often people die long before the coroner pronounces them dead. Had this husband and father died the first day he entered Moab? Perhaps the need to succumb to standards far from those he'd come to value in Bethel contributed to his demise. Did his family note his silence as the man of God said nothing to a culture he'd learned to quietly tolerate? Had he died amid the questions racing through his mind, "What does my wife think of me?" "Have I failed my sons?" Surely, he must have pondered the decision he'd made as he watched his sons become assimilated in cultural values. Though the scripture tells us it happens, no actual date is given when Elimelech, Naomi's husband dies. It is only said that he dies, and she was left. Although she survives her husband, we know a part of Naomi was gone too, but she had her two sons.

Despite their assimilation to a culture they'd learn to call home, Mahlon and Chilion were still her sons. How her heart must have ached to see her sons live so far from the values she wanted them to embrace. The ultimate endorsement of their full assimilation to this wicked culture was when each of her sons took wives of Moab, Ruth, and Orpah. Her sons had succumbed to Moab. Each had covenanted with it in that they had taken wives and could potentially produce offspring of the same culture. Was it the providence of God that no children were born of these unions? Perhaps it was the mercy of God, that Naomi was spared the pain of watching another generation be removed from the values she loved. After 10 years of living in Moab, both of Naomi's sons die. What devastation she must have felt as she realizes that all that brought her any value was gone.

In Part One, I share the importance of being God Made; not allowing any entities outside of God to make us. She now finds herself a widow in a strange land. If she were in Bethlehem, then a relative of her husband would be obligated to take care of her. Considering her options, she inquired of things in Bethlehem and found that there was food there. Having learned that conditions are better in Bethlehem, she decides to go back home. Unlike the famine which years before led to their move to Moab, her hunger, though not physical, is more dreadful. Naomi has lost everything on the earth which she as well as a society felt brought her usefulness and value. Naomi told her two daughter-n-laws, Ruth and Orpah of her decision to go back to Bethlehem. The women agreed to go with her, and the women were in route to Bethlehem when Naomi started to have second thoughts about her decision to allow Ruth and Orpah accompany her. Although she came to love them as her daughters, she now felt it be best for them to depart. She explains to them that she has nothing to offer them and encourages them to return to their families. She assured them that God would deal kindly with them as they had been kind to both she and her sons. Tearfully, the women kissed and embraced each other. Though Ruth and Orpah are so different from Naomi in their cultural views, we find no cultural divides here in suffering lost. Using every argument, Naomi tries to convince her daughter-n- laws to return to their families. Orpah was finally convinced and decided to return home to her family. Despite Naomi's dissuasions, Ruth cleaved the more to her mother-n-law, refusing to return to her family. It's the open brokenness, the nakedness in Naomi which was of most value to her. She didn't realize that it's her nakedness that caused Orpah to weep in sadness as she left her mother-n-law in return to her family. Neither did she know that it was the same exposure that caused Ruth to cleave to her more, despite there being reasons to leave as well.

"In the days when the judges ruled, there was a famine in the land. So a man from Bethlehem in Judah, together with his wife and two sons, went to live for a while in the country of Moab. The man's name was Elimelech, his wife's name was Naomi, and the names of his two sons were Mahlon and Kilion. They were Ephrathites from Bethlehem, Judah. And they went to Moab and lived there. Now Elimelech, Naomi's husband, died, and she was left with her two sons. They married Moabite women, one named Orpah, and the other Ruth. After they had lived there about ten years, both Mahlon and Kilion also died, and Naomi was left without her two sons and her husband. When Naomi heard in Moab that the LORD had come to the aid of his people by providing food for them, she and her daughters-in-law prepared to return home from there. With her two daughters-in-law, she left the place where she had been living and set out on the road that would take them back to the land of Judah. Then Naomi said to her two daughters-in-law, "Go back, each of you, to your mother's home. May the LORD show you kindness, as you have shown kindness to your dead husbands and to me. May the LORD grant that each of you will find rest in the home of another husband." Then she kissed

them goodbye, and they wept aloud and said to her, "We will go back with you to your people." But Naomi said, "Return home, my daughters. Why would you come with me? Am I going to have any more sons, who could become your husbands? Return home, my daughters; I am too old to have another husband. Even if I thought there was still hope for me—even if I had a husband tonight and then gave birth to sons—would you wait until they grew up? Would you remain unmarried for them? No, my daughters. It is more bitter for me than for you because the LORD's hand has turned against me!" At this, they wept aloud again. Then Orpah kissed her mother-in-law goodbye, but Ruth clung to her. "Look," said Naomi, "your sister-in-law is going back to her people and her gods. Go back with her." But Ruth replied, "Don't urge me to leave you or to turn back from you. Where you go, I will go, and where you stay, I will stay. Your people will be my people and your God my God." (Ruth 1:1-16 NIV)

Garments of Shame

It was the shame of being naked which caused Naomi as she entered Bethlehem to greet the people in shame rather than honor. We recognize in Naomi the sense of emptiness we see in many who encounter loss…death, divorce, relocations, or even career changes. When Naomi entered her hometown, the people were moved and questioned among themselves who they would allow her to be. The scrutiny of her identity among her people caused her to reflect more earnestly on her loss. How could she ever be called Naomi again when she'd suffered such lost? Naomi's deprivation would challenge her to accept the truth of who she was in the eyes of society and even her own eyes. She no longer had what made her who she was previously. Though she came back to the place where she started, she is

118

empty, void, and darkness covers her soul.

In Part One, we shared with you this place where creation begins. The earth was dark, void and the spirit moved upon the earth, and God said let there be light. Naomi needed the light of God's wisdom and purpose to illuminate the darkness of her soul so that she could see the light of who He created her to be, and apart from all things she thought gave her value. It was her perception of this complete loss which causes her to refer to herself as Mira, an expression of her condition of mind and being. Not only had she lost everything physically, but she'd also lost her sense of worth. Attributing her lost to God's providence is consistent with the irrational thought that is prevalent in the church today. If good things happen, then we must be in right standing with God, but when adversity comes, then God has dealt harshly with us. It was here that God challenged Naomi 's life view though she struggled to hold on to some dignity (clothing). Fighting against the stares and judgments of those who criticized her for leaving the first place… those who judged that she got only what she deserved; indeed it was God's response to evil; or others who feared that she'd want from them more than they desired or were willing to give. Grabbing whatever clothing she could to cover her shame from the stares, she changes her name saying, "Call me Mara."

Naomi was returning to the only place where God could make of her whom she was destined to become. He couldn't do that with her being lost in all the things that made her Naomi. Although she'd been given this name, circumstances stripped away her identity and left her naked and in shame. How important it is that we see ourselves as nothing apart from God! Naomi struggled and saw herself empty and worthless. It's in utter demise that God pulled out the canvas to have His true image emerge through her. I believe it will be out of such spiritual nakedness that the church will reveal itself as the real bride Christ wants to present to the Father.

Lesson 20
God's Chosen: The Shame and Separation of Nakedness

A Need to Hide

My father was a remarkable preacher. People came from all around when they heard he would be preaching. How proud I was to be the daughter of such an immense figure in his day. Although he stood amiably behind the pulpit as the Word of God resonated through the crowd, he still hid his struggles. I'd watch him sitting at the kitchen table with his head buried in his hands crying out to God warring against the demons of his flesh. Would the crowds have filled up the church if they knew of his struggles? Beyond the church, what would his family say or think of such an appalling disguise? My father died in the pulpit draped in the veneer of greatness. Tears roll down my cheek as I think of the agony and pain he suffered as he wandered more in-depth into the forest hiding among the trees in his nakedness. I'm convinced that our pulpits and churches are filled with those who hide in shame that which Christ came to heal. Jesus knew He'd come as God in the flesh. On one occasion, one came referring to Him as good master and asked, "What good thing shall I do that I may have eternal life?" Jesus immediately addressed the man's assumption, though not spoken, that those who did well were good. Jesus sought to dispel the presumption that He or any other fleshly person could be good. Asserting that only God is good.

"Just then a man came up to Jesus and asked, "Teacher, what good thing must I do to get eternal life?" "Why do you ask me about what is good?" Jesus replied. "There is only One who is good. If you want to

enter life, keep the commandments." (Matthew 19:16-1,7 NIV)

Jesus was not suggesting that good works would not be the response in those who sought life eternally, but rather that works of any kind don't make a man good or evil. Jesus applauds our works proposing that when we do good works, they in and of themselves glorify the Father which is in heaven who is good. Matthew 5:16 (KJV) ...The Apostle Paul speaks to this apparent inconsistency as he describes the inward struggle for good in a fleshly body in Romans 7. We do not condone sin in any wise neither do we suggest that sin is not appalling to God. Sin is indeed wretched, disdained, and poses a vile odor in the nostrils of a Holy God. Regardless of how dreadful our sins, Christ made graceful atonement for them all. Not that any should continue in sin, but that each may be offered a remedy for the shame of nakedness we desperately seek to hide. Does my heart lament the many prominent men and women of God who seek desperately to hide the shame of their nakedness like my father? How long will they choose impressionable fig leaves which propose earthly grandeur while eluding Godly worship?

Come, my friend; join me at the feet of Christ. He invites us to learn of Him. It's here that His image is made clearer and your heart yearns to be more like Him. How long will we bear the yoke of shame and death?

"Come to me, all you who are weary and burdened, and I will give you rest. Take my yoke upon you and learn from me, for I am gentle and humble in heart, and you will find rest for your souls. For my yoke is easy and my burden is light." (Matthew 11:28-30 NIV)

Man's Separation from God

The first couples' nakedness took them farther and farther away from God. As they sought desperately to clothe themselves in the right imagery, the more appealing the trees became. Mark the gospel writer tells of an occasion when Christ enters Bethsaida, a blind man is brought to him to be healed. Christ took the man by the hand, led him out of the town, spit on his eyes, laid hands on him them asked the man what he saw. The man looking up replied, "I see men as trees walking." Jesus touched the man's eyes again, asked him to look up once more. The man's sight being completely restored saw all men (Mark 8:22-25). Have we satisfied ourselves with seeing mankind as trees? Trees more often suggest some deep-rooted foundational truths which will never be removed by cutting away the surface. I hear the wind rustling the trees affirming the impending storms which will radically alter the church as we know it. Perhaps, mankind has lost sight of a Holy God. In exchange, He has been made as unto graven images created through the blinded perceptions of man. Additionally, I sense that few have the fear or reverence of God as He has been reduced to that which is earthly and lowly.

For some time after the fall of man, there was no fear of God. All type of immorality and death was on the earth. Cain's killing of his brother Abel marked the first assault against a fleshly man. This ultimate assault continued until Adam and Eve gave birth to Seth at which time men began to call upon the name of the Lord. The earth will continue in a state of demise until the earth gives birth to those who will not only call for but be guided by the Spirit of a Holy

God. The Prophet Isaiah urges us to seek the Lord and draw near to Him. He proposes that our ways are far from what God intends for those representing His holiness. (Isaiah 55:6-9)

Churches, men, and women who profess to know God continue to call out to a God who appears powerless because our sins have separated us from Him. The Lord is at hand to help, but he purposefully does not help because as the first couple intentionally sought to hide from the Holiness of God, He has in exchange determined to reveal Himself only to those who seek Him diligently with their whole hearts not wanting to be clothed in leaves of deception hid among enticing acclaim.

"Then you will call on me and come and pray to me, and I will listen to you. You will seek me and find me when you seek me with all your heart." (Jeremiah 29:12-13NIV).

A Marred Relationship: The Woman You Gave to Be with Me

Mankind struggle still to accomplish meaningful relationships without the presence of God. How can relationships be meaningful when it's evident that many are flawed? How can good be present when eclipsed with evil? The enemy knew the struggle we'd encounter as we saw good and evil without the presence of a Holy God. Man and woman ran together among the trees, overwhelmed with the awareness of both good and evil, they sought to become one in relationships which were marred. When God called for man's accountability for where he was, it was not to bring shame, but rather to bring him to a place of truthful worship.

"Then the man and his wife heard the sound of the LORD God as he was walking in the garden in the cool of the day, and they hid from the LORD God among the trees of the garden. 9 But the LORD God called to the man, "Where are you?" He answered, "I heard you in the garden, and I was afraid because I was naked; so I hid." (Genesis 3:8-10, NIV)

When God saw a man running among the trees seeking to hide his nakedness, He questioned the authority which told man and woman that they were not enough or were inferior in their present state. God intended that mankind would be blind to gender, race, culture, or doctrine which lend way to judgments and biases. Man sought hard to hide his nakedness from the piercing eyes of God. He was certain it was not enough to cover the defects he saw in his wife. Knowing that he couldn't dispel her from the garden, the man allows the woman to work beside him while devaluing the need for her. Although we will explore the phenomenon of blaming others in the next lesson, I would like to address man's present state of mind which perhaps marred the couple's relationship. Having eaten of the forbidden fruit, man no longer sees the woman as an integral part of his existence as presented in Part One. He no longer welcomed her. She's no longer viewed as needful or as one to be desired in communion with his spiritual wholeness. Their initial sense of oneness is threatened and shattered as he sought to disconnect from one with whom God has joined him. He recognized her connection to him, but sees it as forceful, undesirable and even debased. When God explored his frame of reference, the man suggested that it was the woman who contributed to his flawed personal exposition. He sees her as a complete entity, but one has no conception with him. Man is aware of God's providential nature but questioned his relational consort with a woman.

"The man said, "The woman you put here with me—she gave me some fruit from the tree, and I ate it..." (Genesis 3:12 NIV)

Lesson 21
Beyond Blame, Taking Personal Responsibility

To defray the shame, he felt by my rebellion, my father would often say, "My daughter has fallen with the wrong crowd." Perhaps he could better theorize my demise if he could contribute it to something or someone outside of me. This theory not only presented me as the victim. but also dismissed the possibility of him being judged as the culprit in my outcome in some wise. For a time, he started to resent any of my acquaintances. Without probable cause, he judged them as thoughtless and devious in some form. Since it was someone else's fault that I was the way that I was, I never determined any realistic plan for altering my behavior. I viewed most church folk as phonies who preached and taught one thing at church and lived hypocritical lives away from the church. I thought a few times about changing before coming to myself on the side of the road that Saturday. I even tried to pull myself away from the crowd Daddy said I'd become a part of...Although I intentionally avoided them and many started to withdraw from me, there was still a tendency for me to war with the demons of my soul. Being alone and away from the crowd, even the church is where I determined that the struggle I was having was not emanating from the crowd I was in or had been in, nor was it the church folk who did or didn't live holy lives...the perpetrator was me. I was the source of my deplorable state and I was the only person who could reciprocate any constant changes in my life, with the guidance of the Holy Spirit. Most people fear to be alone. We see the devastation when people die; walk through a divorce; retire from long careers; or even when friendships or relationships of any meaningful kind are challenged. It was when left alone that Jacob struggled with himself and God until he received a breakthrough at daybreak (Genesis 32:24).

Likewise, when left alone in the wilderness Jesus became emancipated from his flesh while being tempted by the devil (Matthew 4:1). Was there some time in the garden that the enemy found the woman alone that he took the occasion to entice her to eat of the forbidden fruit? Although the couple both decided to eat, it was when the woman was alone that the enemy enticed her to conceive the desire to eat. From the beginning of time, we find this need to blame others. When God questioned the man about their nakedness, the man accused the woman, and she blamed the serpent. While the serpent being viewed the culprit, God indicts each individually. God held each responsible for their choices. (Genesis 3:12-19)

When I finally came to myself and came back to the Father's House it was easy for me to be guilty. No matter who did what, it had to be my fault even if I was not present. I kept handy an exhausting list of "if's" which I'd gladly lend any offender. Certainly, my husband or children would not have... if I was a better wife or mother. If I'd been a better teacher or counselor, the students or the school system would be.... If I were a better minister or teacher, more people would get saved. While presenting a case to my husband in my usual "save all" defense he asked, "Who made you God?" I stammered something about not trying to be God, while he relentlessly accused me of being in God's way. My son informed me of his desire to get engaged at Christmas. "What do you think of me getting engaged mom?" he asked. Trying to shield my son from hearing the anxious feeling that was in the pit of my stomach I presented some common marriage queries. We only talked for a few minutes, but it seemed like hours. When he got off the phone, I rushed to my list of "If's" thinking that certainly, I haven't prepared him enough for this serious venture into such a lifelong commitment. I was certain that I didn't want to be left alone at this time. I'd asked him, "What did your Daddy say?" He told me that he hadn't told him yet, but he would. Surprisingly, a smile swept across my face as I heard my soul echo my husband's words, "Who made you, God?" My son did propose, and her parents consented. I shared in their happiness as we facetimed both smiling from ear to ear. I know that there will be valleys and mountains ahead of them, yet, I feel total freedom as I gave them my blessings and asked God to be God. In the irony of blame, there remain those who dare to blame God in the absence of others -to blame for their transgressions. Such accusation is strongly refuted as James recounts the Holiness of God's nature which cannot be tempted by evil or tempt one by the same. James acknowledges the innate presence of evil desires in all of mankind while proposing the powerlessness of sin in the absence of inward appeal. (James 1:13-15)

The Apostle Paul supports man's commonality to temptation in his writing to the Corinthian church, while at the same time offering Jesus as a faithful remedy to those of us desiring to escape the clutches of our sinful nature. (1 Corinthian 10:13) We do have an advocate, Jesus Christ, God in the flesh who is moved by our fleshly struggles as He was tempted as we all are, yet He did not sin. Let us run boldly to Him who extends to us grace and mercy to help us in our times of need.

"For we do not have a high priest who is unable to empathize with our weaknesses, but we have one who has been tempted in every way, just as we are—yet he did not sin. Let us then approach God's throne of grace with confidence, so that we may receive mercy and find grace to help us in our time of need." (Hebrews 4:15-16 NIV)

Second Adam, Christ

God knew from the start that mankind would fall short of His desired glory and He made provisions for it. When He made man, He consulted with every aspect of His being concluding that He would make man in their image (Genesis 1:26). Though man was created to bear the image of a Holy God, he was earthly and lowly. One must always consider that man was made even lower than the angels, but given glory, power, and dominion by God over all the works of His hands.

"For what is mankind that you are mindful of them, human beings that you care for them? You have made them a little lower than the angels and crowned them with glory and honor. You made them rulers over the works of your hands; you put everything under their feet." (Psalm 8:4-6 NIV)

Being given such authority in the earth, Man could easily think himself to be God rather than the bearer of His image. Perhaps it's this innate desire which allures man toward temptation that distinguishes man from God who cannot be tempted. Is there an impending penalty against those who suppose themselves to be lofty or exalted above who they were created to be? The Bible tells us that Lucifer was an

130

angel who desired to be like God even to be exalted above the heaven and desired to establish his throne above the stars, but he was dispelled from heaven to earth. *(Isaiah 14:12-14)*

Satan being in the form of a serpent in the garden appeals to this desire in the woman as he suggests that eating the forbidden fruit will offer that they be as God knowing good and evil rather than just bearing His image (Genesis 3:5). As I suggested earlier in this writing, various aspects of the world, though created, were made manifest at specific times. The first man, Adam through willful disobedience separates us from God…yielding death. All human beings were made partakers of death through this one violation and none could offer a remedy for their broken relationship with God. Since one man caused the deadly separation for all, then it would be practical that one man would then offer restoration and life to all. As a remedy for death, the invisible God was made in the likeness of man and came to earth in the person of Christ to satisfy the penalty of death imposed against humans through the first man, Adam.

"For if, by the trespass of the one man, death reigned through that one man, how much more will those who receive God's abundant provision of grace and the gift of righteousness reign in life through the one man, Jesus Christ!" (Romans 5:17 NIV)

Lesson 22
No Condemnation

An antidote must be applied to obtain the expected results. Jesus came as atonement for the separation imposed upon man. Sadly, many who have not used the atoning blood of Jesus to their lives continue to suffer the guilt, shame and condemnation brought on by the first man's violation. I spent many years trying to pay for the sins of my past. I'd teach and preach about the power of the blood while not applying its cleansing power to my life. It was hard for me to grasp the concept that just as sin and the penalty of death passed to all of humanity by one man, Adam, so was the penalty of death completely removed by the sacrifice of one man, Christ. There was nothing for me, or other believers to do but accept the atonement offered through Christ and live. Although there remains a fleshly nature in us, the Spirit of God empowers us to live a life free from the shadow of guilt and shame which was once our verdict. Jesus knew the heart of the Jews of His day, and He knew how many felt a sense of freedom because they were Abraham's seed. He desperately wanted to teach them and desired that they would receive freedom apart from the law which He offered. Some did believe on Him and accepted His words. He encouraged them to continue in the freedom provided through the truth found in His words. (John 8:31-34)

Ministry allows me the opportunity to often share with people who have been incarcerated. Regardless of the offense or the length of time of their incarceration, I find the same embedded spirit of condemnation. Therefore, it's difficult for them to assimilate back into society though they've served time for their offenses. The prison doors were opened, and each walked out, but none escaped the chains which condemned them to death. It seems that stoning was a common practice imposed against those found guilty of an offense in earlier times. People of our day would be appalled at the thought of such justification. Are demeaning judgments, criticism, slanderous comments hurled at others especially through social media as scornful? With the Bible in one hand and a stone in the other, well-meaning Christians preach a gospel which liberates while at the same time cast condemning stones at those accused. How can freedom be offered to the sinner as he or she is met with stony hearts while walking in the public squares, or more importantly, while sitting in the pews of our churches?

John writes in his gospel of the woman brought to Christ by the scribes and Pharisees having been caught in the act of adultery. Trying to find a reason to accuse him, they expound the law of Moses as it relates to this offense. Knowing that the penalty for the offense was that she should be stoned, Jesus asked that he that was without sin should throw the first stone at the woman. Realizing their sinful nature, each of her accusers walked away. Jesus asked the woman about those who accused her and what was her condemnation. Finding that she had none, Jesus said, "Neither do I condemn you, go and sin no more." The gospel of Christ is saying to the sinner condemned to death, "Go and sin no more, there is none to condemn." (John 8:1-11)

All Things New

Growing up in a poor family allowed me the experience of "making do." There was rarely enough of what we needed, so something else took the place of whatever was thought to be missing. When there was no meat and one of us dared to ask about the meat, momma would say, "You children know that rice stands for meat," as she sat the bowl of rice in front of us. None of us questioned it any. Furthermore, we all grew up thinking that anything available could be substituted for what was lacking. I completed much of this writing at the Prayer House, the name was given to my grandfather's old house which sits in the back of ours. Although some of the community women worked with me to refurbish it, many imperfections; uneven moldings; gaps in the walls and doors and segmented floors are intentionally left as a reminder of this "making do" mentality. Our houses were built by family members who were not real carpenters. Some of them were more skilled at the craft than others, but our financial situation insisted that we made things work when the proper things were not available. I'm looking now at a piece of wood over the door, its edges are rough and a misfit for its purpose. I can imagine the conversation my grandfather had while nailing it up, "Boy get me something to go right here over this door." My dad or uncle probably ran outside and got whatever piece of wood they thought was suitable and brought it back. No one even cut the edges that were too long or uneven; they just nailed it up.

Years have passed since my grandfather's house was built. I kept much of the house in its original form, but a few things we did replace. For too long we have operated under a "make do" type gospel. We've taken whatever works best to build the constructs of the church. Like the wood over the door, some principles serve as reminders of what was and how everybody substituted rice for meat without question. The Apostle Paul was writing to the Corinthians who were given to an old system of worldly living. He'd presented them the gospel of Christ but knew that they would easily incorporate certain practices into their new life if they were not cautioned. He urged them to embrace the newness of Christ and let go of the old. He told them that they are now a part of the family of God and that they are new creations. Old things must be removed for the new things to appear. (2 Corinthians 5:17)

The Apostle further urges other churches that they do the same- Put off the corruptions and deeds of their former nature brought on by inward lust. He does this when he refers to them as the old man and put on the new man who is renewed through the Spirit of God through the mind. (Ephesians 4:22-23) It's not needful that I change the total infrastructure of my grandfather's old house, but it's essential that I have a new way of looking at it. I can't keep the mindset of "make do" when something new is needful and available. There are no substitutes for what Christ did for us on the cross. A life of works will never satisfy the requirements of sinful death. Before Jesus came, all we had was the reminder of our sinful nature brought on by the law. In Romans, the Apostle Paul describes man's dual nature. On the one hand, man knows what is right and wants desperately to do it. Also, man knows what is wrong and wants desperately not to do it, yet he finds another nature in him warring against his will to perform righteously and avoid evil. The Apostle concludes that aside from substitutes or "make do" solutions, only Christ offers the cure for such soul schizophrenia.

Lesson 23
Be Fruitful and Multiply

Fruitfulness has always been God 's desire for mankind. When God created man and woman, He commanded that they be fruitful and multiply in the earth. He desired that the earth would be filled with those possessing and understanding His Spiritual nature. He did this to the extent that he and she could through Him, defeat anything presenting as living things that challenged His ultimate authority in the earth.   He desired that man reproduced in the earth those knowing who He was and found life and even the abundance of life through Him. (John 10:10) There has never been a problem with a man having an abundance of life. God only requires that man remains aware that all life comes through Him and Him alone. When man allowed the earth (flesh nature) to rule over him, God determined that He would destroy man from the face of the earth. Howbeit one man, Noah found grace in the sight of God and He and his family were spared from God's destruction of the earth. God determined that He would never again curse the earth or destroy it regardless of man's sinful nature. God blessed Noah and his sons and commanded that they again be fruitful in the earth and replenish it after the flood. (Genesis 9:1)

Following the flood, God 's desire continues to be man 's fruitfulness. He established a covenant with Abraham when he was 91 years old saying if he walked in obedience to Him, He'd allow him to be exceedingly fruitful with nations and even kings descending from his bowels. (Genesis 17:6) Because Abraham obeyed God, his seed was blessed after him. Not only was Isaac fruitful, so was Jacob. God promised him and his seed after him the land he'd given to his fathers… Abraham and Isaac. (Genesis35:12)

The Prophet Jeremiah prophesied of a time that the sheep would be scattered by the shepherds, pastors who have "made do" with the gospel. God's people as sheep are scattered upon every hillside and bellowing for the shepherds to come and feed them. I believe the church is entering the hour where the Lord will gather a remnant of men and women from the many places that he has allowed them to be scattered. He will assemble them as one people serving one God and will raise up shepherds after His own heart, as David, to feed them. (Jeremiah 23:1-8) Not only will the church be fruitful again in number, but those who serve will also be filled with good works through the knowledge and constructs of a Holy God.

You...Go be fruitful and multiply in His good works... in His image.

PART III

LESSON REVIEW

LIFE CHANGING TRUTHS

- The Father's House- The Master promises us a place with Him and the Father if we only believe. Although we do not deserve it, He extends to us a ring and a robe, signifying an everlasting covenant with Believers.

- Naked and not Ashamed- It takes much courage to be willing to be exposed, yet it's this vulnerable state which allows others to see more of the image of God.

- A Need to Hide- I suggest that there are astounding numbers of members who fill our churches Sunday after Sunday who ascribes to mask their struggles beneath thunderous sermons, prayers, and songs in their attempt to hide aimlessly from God.

- True Worship- It's easy to go to church even lift our hands seemingly in worship and still not be in true covenant with God. True Worship comes only as one acknowledges the truth in the inward parts.

- None Good but the Father- Our good deeds are simply our response to a Holy God and will never in and of themselves make us good because God alone is good.

- Marred Relationships- Mankind was created not only for a communal relationship with God but also with one another. When relationships are marred in either context, then God's unconditional grace and mercy are prohibited.

- Beyond Blame- Mankind must admit that we are the source of our own deplorable state, take responsibility for our own choices, and reciprocate perpetual life changes with the guidance of the Holy Spirit.

- No Condemnation- God being made in the likeness of man came to earth in the person of Christ to satisfy the penalty of death imposed against humans through the first man, Adam.

As a result of his sacrifice, we have been redeemed from death and can live our lives free from all shame and condemnation.

- All Things New- Those of us who have accepted the atonement offered through Christ are now "New Creations." We have been freed from our old lives despite its corruption and can now live righteous lives trusting in the finished work of Christ.

- Be Fruitful and Multiply- Fruitfulness is not only God's desire but His command for mankind. He desires that man reproduce in the earth those knowing who He is and finds life... even the abundance of life through Him.

ABOUT THE AUTHOR

Minister Jo Ann Shealey grew up and currently resides in rural Cottage Grove, AL (Coosa County). She grew up in the "church world" with her father having served as pastor of two churches. She is married to Rev. Larry Shealey, Pastor of Darian Baptist Church in Alexander City, AL, and is the mother of two children: Larrecia and Larry Jr. She has a BS in Education obtained from Alabama A & M University, Huntsville, AL and an MA in School Counseling from Troy University/Montgomery.

Minister Shealey has been conferred with many honorary awards and participates in various community and civic organizations. She is the Director of Warrior Women's Ministry (Darian Baptist Church), Founder of House of Prayer, a prayer and intercessory group, Coosa County Children Policy Council member, and teacher in the Early Rose Congress of Christian Education.

Minister Shealey works as a part-time parent-teacher facilitator with SAFE/Sylacauga. This position allows her the opportunity to empower pregnant women and mothers with parenting skills, and children's development knowledge. She is a retired teacher/school counselor with Coosa County School System (30.5 years of service) and has been a licensed Minister since 1996. She conducts a bi-annual intensive women discipleship training "And He Called Her Woman" where many women have embraced their God-given purpose.

Minister Shealey has enjoyed serving in ministry with her husband for the last 28 years at Darian Baptist Church. She is a conference/motivational speaker, writer, and storyteller. Like Christ, she uses parables to communicate the truth of God's Word, making it inviting and meaningful to all people of ages. She has received many awards and honors. Her most recent one being the 2018 Humanitarian Award given in recognition of her service to women and families. However, she ascribes her greatest accomplishments as being in the family of God, and to have His trust to Minister His Word, leading many to a personal relationship with Him.

ABOUT THE

CONTRIBUTING AUTHOR

Dr. Tomeka W. McGhee received her doctorate from Auburn University in Counselor Education and Supervision and a Master's degree in Counseling and Psychology from Troy University. She is an engaging and reflective counselor educator, licensed professional counselor, nationally certified counselor, licensed minister, facilitator, speaker, and author. As a facilitator, she adeptly and intuitively leads group experiences ranging from grief and loss to cultural humility for personal and professional enrichment. Clinically, her work involves creating safe, sacred, and transformative spaces by which individuals and groups can explore life-giving ways of being, through a holistic wellness framework.

In her 10 years of experience as a therapist, Dr. Tomeka McGhee has worked with adults in career development as a global career development facilitator (GCDF) and adults and children in the areas of severe and chronic mental illness and trauma. She works with issues concerning grief and loss, depression, anxiety, life transition, spirituality, relationships, and conducts clinical assessments/evaluations and group counseling for other mental health and social service agencies in private practice. Outside her clinical and higher education work, she has long served her community as a licensed minister, Area Director of a youth organization, newspaper columnist, mental health consultant, workshop provider, and Governance Chairwoman of the Tallapoosa County Children's Policy Council.

Extending beyond the local community, she has extensive service to the counseling profession in state and regional capacities such as President of the Alabama Counseling Association, President of the Alabama Association of Counselor Educators and Supervisors, Executive Conference Committee Member of the Southern Association for Counselor Educators and Supervisors, along with numerous conference presentations and professional association memberships.

Her most prized work is being a wife of 25 years to Tracy McGhee and mother to Gabriel, Nicolas, and Trinity McGhee. She enjoys reading challenging and life-giving spiritual literature, times of contemplation in silence and solitude in nature, near a body of water, or at her favorite Benedictine Monastery, and new adventures.

ABOUT THE PUBLISHER

CoolBird Publishing House is a division of
CoolBird Marketing, LLC and is nestled away in the small quaint town
of Goodwater, Alabama. To learn more about
CoolBird Publishing House and our services, visit:

CoolBird Publishing House
PO BOX 612
Goodwater, AL 35072

www.coolbirdpublishinghouse.com
1.888.588.3764

Made in the USA
Columbia, SC
29 August 2023